ROMAN
PUBLIC BUILDINGS

ROMAN
PUBLIC BUILDINGS

Edited by I. M. Barton

EXETER STUDIES IN HISTORY No. 20

First published by the University of Exeter 1989.

EXETER STUDIES IN HISTORY

General Editors   Jonathan Barry and Colin Jones

Editorial Committee

David Braund	Michael Duffy
Robert Higham	Malyn Newitt

Printed and bound by Short Run Press Ltd, Exeter

ISBN 0 85989 239 5
ISSN 0260 8628

Contents

List of Figures, Maps and Plates

iv

LIST OF FIGURES, MAPS AND PLATES

II. Plates (located between pp. 84 and 85)

LIST OF FIGURES, MAPS AND PLATES

34. Aspendos, aqueduct: one of the so-called 'pressure towers'

35. Rome, Aqua Marcia. Model of the Ponte Lupo

36. Rome, Aqua Claudia: the arcade carrying the aqueduct across the Campagna

37. Rome, Aqua Claudia: arcade with brick liner added, to strengthen the arches and seal leaks

38. Rome, Porta Maggiore

39. Nemausus, *castellum divisorium*

40. Montpellier (France): eighteenth-century *château d'eau* du Peyrou

III. *Maps*

Abbreviations

AE	*L'Année épigraphique*
AJA	American Journal of Archaeology
ANRW	*Aufstieg und Niedergang der römischen Welt*
CQ	Classical Quarterly
ILLRP	*Inscriptiones Latinae Liberae Rei Publicae*
ILS	*Inscriptiones Latinae Selectae*
JRS	Journal of Roman Studies
LACTOR	London Association of Classical Teachers: The Classical Association
MEFR	*Mélanges d'Archéologie et d'Histoire de l'Ecole française de Rome*
PBSR	Papers of the British School at Rome
PLRE	Prosopography of the Later Roman Empire

Acknowledgements

My first thanks go to the Editorial Committee of the Exeter Studies in History series for commissioning this volume, and to David Braund and Peter Wiseman for their encouragement and help. I am grateful to my fellow-contributors for their ready cooperation in providing their chapters and for their patience in awaiting the publication. I acknowledge with gratitude grants from the Pantyfedwen Trust of Saint David's University College towards the cost of typing and illustrations. Diana Catley, Maureen Hunwicks and Ceinwen Jones undertook typing and word-processing at various stages, and I am grateful for their help. Thanks also to Alan Rogers for expert advice and practical help with the technicalities of computer typesetting.

The following have kindly given permission for the reproduction of copyright material:

Figures

B.T. Batsford Limited and Frank Sear: 17, 18, 19, 23, 25, from F. Sear, *Roman architecture* (London 1982); B.T. Batsford Limited and John H. Humphrey: 42, from J.H. Humphrey, *Roman circuses* (London 1986); Société d'Edition Les Belles Lettres, Paris: 48; Professor F. Castaglioni: 1, 6; Chatto & Windus and Iain Browning: 38, from I. Browning, *Jerash and the Decapolis* (London 1982); Amanda Claridge: 14, 34, from *Pompeii A.D. 79*

(London 1976); Ecole des Hautes Etudes, Paris: 2; Sheila Gibson: 11; The University of Michigan Press: 4, 24, from F. Brown, *Cosa: the Making of a Roman Town* (Ann Arbor 1980); Società nazionale di scienze lettere e arti in Napoli: 37; Musées d'art et d'histoire, Nîmes: 47; Penguin Books Limited and the Estate of Axel Boëthius, copyright 1970 and 1978: 3, 15, 16, 26, from A. Boëthius, *Etruscan and Roman Architecture* (Harmondsworth 1978); Penguin Books Limited and the Estate of J.B. Ward-Perkins, copyright 1970 and 1981: 21, 22, 30, 31, 32, 39, 40, 41, from J.B. Ward-Perkins, *Roman Imperial Architecture* (Harmondsworth 1981); The Rainbird Publishing Group Limited: 7, 8, 9, 10, 12, 13 ©Rainbird Reference Books Ltd, 1977; Editions A. & J. Picard, Paris: 43, 49, 50(b); Scientific American: 44; Dr Norman Smith: 45; Ernst Wasmuth Verlag Tübingen: 28, from P. Zanker, *Forum Augustum* (Tübingen 1978); Yale University Press: 20, from W. MacDonald, *Architecture of the Roman Empire.* I. (New Haven, Connecticut 1965).

Plates

Ian Barton: 11, 14, 16, 19, 20; The British School at Rome: 2; Tony Brothers: 4, 8, 17, 22, 23, 24, 25, 26, 27, 28, 32, 39; Fototeca Unione, at the American Academy in Rome: 1, 5, 6, 7, 9, 10, 12, 15, 18, 29; Dipl.-Ing. K. Grewe, Rheinisches Amt für Bodendenkmalpflege: 30; Trevor Hodge: 31, 36, 37, 39; Bill Manning: 13; Museo della civiltà romana, Rome: 35; Eddie Owens: 3; Spanish National Tourist Office: 33; Statens Museum for Kunst, København: 21.

To all of the above I am extremely grateful, and I apologise for any inadvertent omissions.

Introduction

IAN M. BARTON

Architecture is the most social of the visual arts. From the megaliths of Stonehenge to the high-rise office blocks of our own day, we can tell a lot about the preoccupations of a society from looking at the buildings it has erected. The Doric and Ionic temples of classical Greece, the piazzas, colonnades and theatres of the Hellenistic world, the great basilicas and bath buildings of the Roman Empire, the cathedrals and castles of the Middle Ages, the palaces and churches of Renaissance Italy, the town halls, libraries and museums of Victorian England: these are just a few examples drawn from European history of classes of buildings which help to bring before our minds a picture of the societies which created them. It is therefore wholly appropriate that a series entitled 'Studies in History' should include a survey of the architecture of a civilisation whose ideas and achievements lie at the root of much of the subsequent political and social development of the countries of western Europe and the Mediterranean.

Why Roman *public* buildings? For a rounded architectural picture of a society we should surely look at their domestic buildings too, from the hovels of peasants to the palaces of monarchs; and indeed the domestic architecture of the Roman Empire is a fascinating study in itself, embracing the great imperial palaces like Nero's Golden House (*Domus Aurea*) and Diocletian's fortress-palace at Split in Dalmatia; country houses of the aristocracy like Pliny's Laurentine villa[1] and Cogidubnus' palace at Fishbourne; town houses ranging from comfortable middle-class residences to shops and slum tenements at places like Pompeii, Ostia and Lepcis Magna; the barrack blocks of legionary fortresses and auxiliary forts; and the great variety of dwellings on working farms which are included under the general term 'villas'. But to attempt to deal adequately with all these as well as public buildings would have increased this book to an unmanageable size; perhaps there will be an opportunity later to add a volume on domestic buildings to the series.

Public architecture at least presents us with the official view of a society and provides the background against which its individual members live their lives; indeed, in certain respects it controls the way in which they spend their time—as participants in political processes, as spectators at entertainments, as worshippers at religious ceremonies, and so on. Roman public buildings may conveniently be divided into three main groups: religious buildings (temples and shrines), buildings for entertainment (theatres, amphitheatres and circuses) and buildings provided for general political, social or economic purposes. In this last group the most striking types are the basilica and the bath building, but it also includes such structures as council chambers (*curiae*), markets and libraries. These groups form the subjects of the three central chapters of this book. They are preceded by a chapter on Roman town planning, which sets the scene for the detailed examination of the different types of building. The last chapter deals with a topic which is closely connected with, and indeed indispensable to, that of public architecture: the water supply of Roman towns, which was always regarded as a prime responsibility of the civic authorities, and without which the cities of Italy and the provinces, to say nothing of the capital, could never have developed as they did.

The main source of our knowledge of Roman buildings is of course the surviving remains of the structures themselves. A few of these are in an almost complete state of preservation: the Pantheon in Rome and the temple known as the 'Maison Carrée' at Nîmes in Provence are the outstanding examples. Others, though no longer complete, are sufficiently well preserved to give a clear idea of their original appearance: the Colosseum (Flavian amphitheatre) in Rome and several of the buildings at Pompeii come into this category. Or they may have continued in use with alterations or have been incorporated into later structures in such a way as to preserve much of their original construction: examples of this in Rome are the Tabularium (public record office), Trajan's market and the great hall of the Baths of Diocletian. In other cases there may be only slight remains, or the building may have disappeared from view entirely as a result either of the abandonment of the site or of the erection of later buildings on it. The latter is much more frequent, since very many Roman towns underlie their mediaeval and modern successors. In such cases modern archaeological investigation has often succeeded in recovering at least the plans of buildings, and sometimes also enough of the superstructure to make possible at least a tentative reconstruction on paper.

There are also references in Latin writers to buildings, especially those in Rome itself, which may give us valuable information about their history. Livy, for example, in his account of the early history of Rome, gives us the traditional foundation dates of many of the temples, and in later books records such innovations as the introduction of Greek architectural ornaments (cf. p. 70) or the construction of the first porticoes in Italy (cf. p. 38). Other examples will be found in the following chapters. Such literary references often inform us of the existence of buildings of which no trace now exists: it is from Tacitus' account of the rebellion of Boudicca[2] that we learn that the newly-founded colony at Camulodunum (Colchester) already had a *curia* and a theatre by A.D. 60; and only the writings of St Cyprian, bishop of Carthage in the middle of the third century, attest the existence of a Capitolium there at that date.[3]

For the theoretical basis of Roman architecture we have one source of paramount importance in the treatise written by Vitruvius.[4] We know nothing about him except what he tells us himself: that he was a practising architect and engineer who had served with Julius Caesar and later helped with the building of one of Augustus' new colonies in Italy, Fanum Fortunae on the Adriatic coast. He must therefore have been an older contemporary of Augustus, to whom he addressed his *Ten Books on Architecture* very early in the emperor's reign. His handbook is a very valuable document. Not only is it the sole surviving work of its kind from antiquity (though we know, largely from a list given by Vitruvius himself, that a number of his more famous predecessors had written about their own architectural achievements or practice). It also happens to have been written at an important point in the development of imperial architecture, when the technical and political conditions necessary to bring that architecture into existence had come about. In Vitruvius we can see the base, so to speak, on which the impressive edifice of urban sophistication and convenience which characterises the Roman empire was raised.

It is obvious from many parts of his work that Vitruvius was influenced by Hellenistic architectural theory. The inhabitants of Italy in the last two centuries B.C. were anxious to show themselves as full and worthy members of the cultural community which stretched from the Pillars of Hercules to the Syrian desert and beyond. Greece was the acknowledged leader in the visual arts, in music, in mathematical and scientific knowledge, in literature, philosophy and oratory. And so it is that we find Vitruvius' work dominated by Greek theory and example, in spite of being firmly anchored in the practical world of late Republican and early Imperial Rome. As a man who had helped to build a 'new town' for Augustus' discharged soldiers, he knew what he was talking about when he discussed the public buildings that were required. As an architect in a tradition that went back at least to the sixth century B.C., he was proud of his knowledge of his Greek predecessors' work and of their theoretical prescriptions. Vitruvius gives us an invaluable picture of the state of Roman architecture on the eve of its most rapid development and dissemination throughout the provinces of the Empire.

The impetus for this came from the extensive programme of rebuilding and new construction undertaken in the city of Rome by Augustus, evidence for which is to be found in the document which he himself drew up as an account of his achievements, the *Res Gestae*.[5] In sections 19–21 of that work he gives a list of some twenty new buildings for which he was responsible, as well as a number of public works which he restored, including no fewer than eighty-two temples (cf. p. 76). Suetonius, recording Augustus' famous claim that he had found Rome a city of brick and left it a city of marble (*'marmoream se relinquere, quam latericiam accepisset'*),[6] mentions a few of these and goes on to add the important information that he encouraged other leading senators to erect buildings on their own account; in particular Marcus Agrippa was responsible for a number of splendid buildings.[7]

Another important source of information about buildings in Rome derives from the building programme of a later emperor, Septimius Severus (193–211). Having ordered an extensive campaign of repairs and restoration of buildings in the capital, Severus had an accurate marble plan of the city (known as the *Forma Urbis*) prepared and set up in one of the halls in Vespasian's Temple of Peace (p. 88).[8] Considerable fragments of this plan have been found; it is sufficiently detailed to enable the plans of some lost buildings to be recovered (p. 70).

Finally, mention must be made of the information provided by inscriptions. Every public building in the Roman world bore at least one inscribed statement, placed usually over the main entrance, which recorded its dedication and the names of its donors (often the municipal authority). Some of these inscriptions are quite lengthy and include a description of the building; frequently they contain a reference to the reigning emperor, by the form of whose title it may be possible to assign a close date to the building. In some instances further inscriptions record later repairs or additions to the building. One example must suffice here: the Antonine Baths, which are the most extensive Roman remains on the site of Carthage. An inscription of A.D. 145 or shortly after[9] records permission given by the emperor Antoninus Pius for the building of the complex and the necessary provision of a water supply; although it is fragmentary, it appears to state that a financial contribution was made from imperial funds. A frieze block from one end of the entablature over the main entrance has also been found,[10] and since it was inscribed on both faces it gives us both the beginning and the end of the dedicatory inscription, from which we learn that the building was dedicated 'for the welfare' (*pro salute*) of the joint emperors Marcus Aurelius and Lucius Verus by the proconsul of Africa in the year 162. Much later a secondary inscription[11] was added on the architrave below, recording that restoration work had been carried out in the time of the emperor Theodosius, between 388 and 390.

There is, then, a substantial body of evidence, and one which is continually increasing, for the history of Roman architecture in general and of individual buildings. How that evidence can be applied will be seen from the chapters which follow.

NOTES

1. Pliny, *Letters* 2.17.

2. Tacitus, *Annals* 14.32.

3. *Letters* 59.13.3; *de lapsis* 8; 24.

4. This and the following paragraph have been written by J.M.Carter. The most convenient text and translation of Vitruvius is by F.Granger in the Loeb Classical Library (2 vols, 1934).

5. Text and translation, with introduction and commentary, by P.A.Brunt and J.M. Moore (Oxford, 1967).

6. Suetonius, *Divus Augustus* 28.3.

7. Id. 29.5.

8. Published by G.Carettoni et al., *La Pianta marmorea di Roma antica* (2 vols, Rome, 1960), supplemented by E. Rodriguez-Almeida, *Forma urbis marmorea: aggiornamento generale 1980* (Rome 1981). New evidence suggests that there was an earlier edition of the plan, perhaps made for Vespasian.

9. ILS 345.

10. AE 1949. 27.

11. Ibid. 28. For the date, see PLRE, Polemius 5.

1. Roman Town Planning

E.J. Owens

Rome itself, like many of the towns of Italy, remained unplanned, the product of unrestricted growth with all its advantages and disadvantages.[1] Yet Rome shared with both the Greeks and the Etruscans a common tradition of urban life which meant that she actively encouraged the growth of new cities. Consequently, as Rome expanded first of all in Italy and later throughout the Mediterranean and Europe, new towns and cities were founded for purposes of military security, administrative efficiency and economic exploitation, and of course to assist the process of Romanisation. The need to create cities, often in areas in which the tradition of urban life was non-existent, brought the Romans face to face with the practical difficulties of urban planning.

Roman town planning began with the conquest of Italy. Colonies were established initially in central Italy and subsequently throughout the peninsula in order to protect Roman territory and to secure conquered lands. In the urbanised parts of Italy new colonists could merely be included in existing towns, although often this was also accompanied by some remodelling. If however an existing town was not suitable, or in those areas of the empire without a tradition of urban life, a new town had to be created. It was then that the Romans faced the practical problems of how this could be achieved. They solved the problem by developing a standard urban design which was based on a regular grid pattern. The developed plan, usually with a square or oblong perimeter and two dominant, centrally intersecting axes, was simple yet effective and Rome applied it repeatedly in creating new towns not only in Italy but also throughout the empire.

Colonisation provided the impetus to town planning but Roman planning did not develop in isolation. In conquering central and southern Italy the Romans came into direct contact with the Greeks and the Etruscans, both of whom already had a long tradition of city building. Indeed for a time Rome had even come under the control of the Etruscans. Cicero records the boasts of the Campanians regarding the healthiness, orderliness and beauty of their cities; and the comparison between Capua, admirably laid out on a flat plain, and Rome with its hills, hanging garrets and poor roads is just one indication of the wealth of planning experience which was available in Italy to the Romans through the efforts of the Greeks and the Etruscans.[2] Before the arrival of the Greeks there was no tradition of planning in Italy.

The emergence of Greece out of the dark age which had followed the collapse of the Mycenaean civilisation had been accompanied by new ideas and fresh initiatives. The incipient *poleis* of the Aegean were unplanned. The rugged, hilly sites, chosen for their defensive capacity, rarely provided the opportunity for systematic planning, and indeed the low level of population, often living in scattered hamlets, precluded the need.[3] However, experiments in new forms of urban design were taking place as the opportunity arose. Old Smyrna, destroyed by fire at the end of the eighth century B.C., was given a new more regular design when it was rebuilt. It is even possible that parts of Miletos were also replanned at about the same time. In establishing colonies the situation was different. New towns of the Greek model had to be created where previously none had existed; and the flat coastal plains of Sicily and southern Italy, chosen for their fertility and agricultural potential, offered opportunities for planning which were not available in the rugged sites of the Aegean.

Megara Hyblaea in Sicily is one of the earliest examples of Greek colonial planning in the West, the layout dating to its initial foundation or shortly after. Then followed Sicilian Naxos. These early experiments in town planning were simple, but they were refined in the course of the seventh and the sixth centuries B.C. into a standard gridded pattern of intersecting broad avenues and narrow streets. Poseidonia, situated in rich, agricultural land on the Campanian coast south of Salerno, represents established Greek planning methods at the end of the sixth century B.C. A wide strip of land running down the centre of the site was reserved for the town's public buildings (fig. 1). It was here that the temples and probably the agora of the original Greek colony were situated, and subsequently,

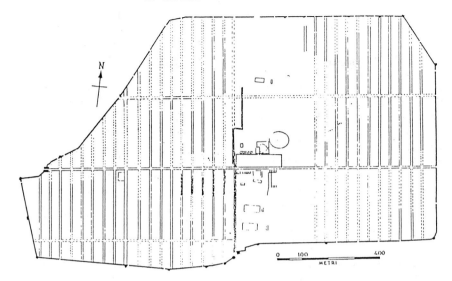

Fig. 1: Plan of Poseidonia (Paestum).

when Poseidonia (renamed Paestum) was recolonised by the Romans in 273 B.C., other buildings including a forum and an amphitheatre were added. Either side of the civic area two residential districts were laid out. The earlier one to the west comprised three widely spaced avenues running in an east-west direction. The line of the two northernmost avenues was continued across the eastern domestic quarter. At right angles to these arterial roads numerous narrower cross streets produced characteristically elongated house blocks (*insulae*). Only later in the course of the fourth century B.C. were the town walls added. The layout of Poseidonia with its distinct residential and public areas and its characteristic grid of streets was repeated throughout the colonies of southern Italy and Sicily, and its pattern laid the foundations for the development of regular planning in central and northern Italy which was taken up by the Etruscans.

The influence of Greek methods on Etruscan practice can be seen in the Etruscan colony at Marzabotto in northern Italy. The town, which takes its name from the modern neighbouring village, lies on the flood plain of the River Reno to the south west of Bologna and was established at the very end of the sixth century B.C. It was laid out as three broad east-west avenues and perpendicular to these ran one north-south avenue and numerous narrower streets (fig. 2). The resulting residential *insulae* are elongated rectangles of characteristically Greek type. However, other aspects of the

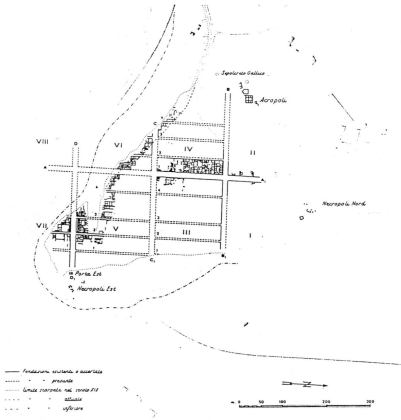

Fig. 2: Plan of the Etruscan town at Marzabotto.

town plan are not Greek and suggest that the Etruscans did not merely copy Greek ideas but made a positive and independent contribution to planning in Italy. The layout of Marzabotto emphasises the intersection of the two central roads, a trend further confirmed by the discovery beneath the junction of the central cross road of a stone inscribed with two lines corresponding to the direction of the two main streets. The hill on the north-western side of the town probably acted as the colony's acropolis, or more correctly its *arx*. The city's major temples were situated here on the same alignment as the lower town. The whole plan subtly combines the different elements of the city in a way uncharacteristic of the Greek colonies in the south.[4] Certainly the comprehensive drainage system, the water supply to the citadel, and the paved roads with raised pedestrian walkways are an indication of the achievements of Etruscan engineering, which was later taken up by the Romans, and an important area of originality in Etruscan planning.

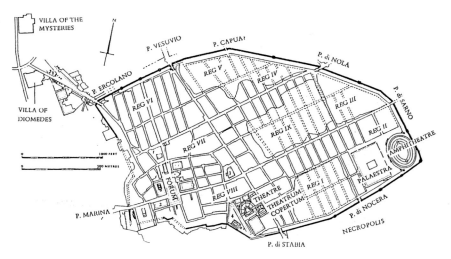

Fig. 3: Plan of Pompeii (1. Forum Baths; 2. Basilica; 3. Stabian Baths; 4. Greek Temple).

Marzabotto together with a few other colonies represents the northern limits of Etruscan influence and penetration. The Etruscans also expanded southwards into Latium and Campania, and it was in the Campanian region in particular that they came into contact with the Greeks. Ideas as well as goods were undoubtedly exchanged and it was this cross-fertilisation of ideas and methods in the cities of Campania which probably laid the foundations of Roman planning. Of the Campanian cities Pompeii exemplifies the interaction of Greek and Etruscan planning methods to which later Roman ideas and specific urban buildings were added. The original Oscan centre, which occupies only the south-western corner of the later city, was small and unplanned. In the course of the fifth century B.C. the city was greatly increased in size by the addition of a series of approximately rectangular extensions (fig. 3). The basis of the new layout was two parallel east-west streets, the Via dell'Abbondanza and the Via di Nola, and a north-south arterial road, the Via di Stabia, which was not exactly perpendicular to the above streets. The districts of the town developed in relation to these streets and consequently the residential *insulae* differ in area, size and shape. Nevertheless the city forms a coherent unit (pl. 1).

As Pompeii grew so public buildings were added. The majority of them are of Roman date, or at least were refurbished in the Roman period, and cluster in three areas of the town in particular: around the forum, in the vicinity of the so-called triangular forum, and in the south-eastern corner of the city. The public buildings around the forum are the most diversified, indicating its importance as a political, legal, religious, social and to a lesser extent economic centre. They include the forum itself with basilica, several temples and close by a food market. The triangular forum was a centre of cultural life and its associated buildings include a theatre and smaller covered *odeion*, and again several temples. The buildings on the south-eastern side of the city were for relaxation and entertainment. Here stood a large Greek style *palaestra* (exercise ground) with a swimming pool of Augustan date, and the earliest known amphitheatre in the Roman world (cf. pp. 114f). In addition to several private baths there were also three public bathing establishments. One of the notable features of Pompeii is the well made roads with raised pedestrian pavements reminiscent of the streets of Marzabotto. There was a comprehensive drainage system and the town was well supplied with water. An aqueduct brought water to a point immediately inside the city wall from where it was distributed to small street fountains, private houses and other buildings throughout the town. The provision of basic amenities was just one area in which Rome improved the quality of life in the cities of the empire.[5]

The history of the urban development of Pompeii is complex. The town, as preserved by the eruption of Vesuvius in A.D.79, is an amalgamation of Greek, Etruscan and Roman efforts. The exact contribution of the Greeks and the Etruscans to the development of the original plan is difficult to disentangle with certainty. Nevertheless it is clear that the combined experience of the Greeks and the Etruscans laid the foundations of Roman planning. The Roman colony of Cosa (Ansedonia) represents the product of their experience.

The colony was planted in 273 B.C. and occupies a rocky site on the coast of Etruria 85 miles north-west of Rome. Despite the difficulties of the site the plan reveals a high degree of unity and skilfully combines the military and civil requirements of the colony (fig. 4). The town walls date from the foundation of the city and make full use of the defensive nature of the terrain, although in so doing they produce an irregular perimeter. Even so the street plan is rectangular and fully co-ordinated with the defences. The gates were reduced to three in number.[6] Of the main roads leading from these gates the two thoroughfares from the north-eastern and south-

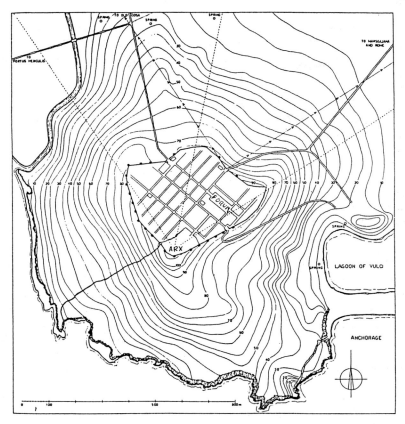

Fig. 4: Plan of the Roman colony of Cosa. The principal temples, including the Capitolium, stood on the citadel (*arx*).

eastern gates meet at right angles approximately in the centre of the town. The other road runs from the north-western gate and the adjacent public building across the city to the forum. Another street runs around the inside of the defences in the manner of a 'pomerial' road. Instead of locating the forum in the centre of the city the planners removed it to more level ground to the south-east, close to the gate and the road leading to the harbour, a position recommended by Vitruvius.[7] Temples stood on the hill (*arx*) overlooking the south-western side of the city, whilst another public building, variously identified as a temple or a granary, has been found close to the north-western gate.[8]

Cosa is proof of the skill of early Roman planners in applying the grid pattern to such a difficult site. As the Romans expanded in Italy the level coastal and riverine sites offered better opportunities for regular planning. Although the colonies which were planted throughout northern and central Italy were in the same tradition as Cosa, they diverged markedly from it in detail and consequently in overall design. In Roman colonies the perimeter was usually extremely regular with either a square or an oblong shape. The street plan laid considerably more emphasis on the two main roads which led from the gates and crossed at the centre of the town. These roads are usually termed the *decumanus maximus* and the *kardo maximus*, corresponding to the main east-west and north-south axes respectively. The forum was situated at this junction. The internal *insulae* in turn tended to be square or oblong, reflecting the overall shape of the town.

The design had already been formulated when the small citizen colony at Ostia was established at the end of the fourth century B.C. some decades before the foundation of Cosa. The original colony now lies under the later town which was developed as Rome's port, but sufficient details have been preserved to indicate that the original colony was rectangular in shape and had two intersecting axial roads. This simple scheme was repeated in Rome's colonies throughout northern and central Italy. At Placentia (Piacenza) the perimeter was square; at Comum (Como) it was oblong. Sometimes geographical considerations brought variations. Internally, however, the design of these towns is the same. The forum occupies a central position where the two arterial roads leading from the gates met. The rest of the town is laid out as a series of square or almost square *insulae*. All the buildings respect the grid unless they were too large and then they were located outside the walls.

Of the factors which influenced the development of this type of grid pattern, military considerations and land surveying are probably the most important.[9] The nature of army camps of the Republican period remains obscure. Indeed Frontinus maintains that it was not until the Romans had overrun the camp of Pyrrhus that they developed an orderly arrangement for their own army camps.[10] Polybius, moreover, compares the orderly arrangement of Roman military camps (fig. 5) to regularly planned towns, implying the priority of the latter.[11] Nevertheless the colonies were overtly military. They were planted in the wake of victorious Roman armies for reasons of security and consequently there is a close relationship between the military and civil requirements of the towns. The defences are fully co-ordinated with the street system, which includes a 'pomerial' road. The gates, always the weak point in fortifications, are reduced to one per side. Certainly in later colonies the military considerations underlying their plan

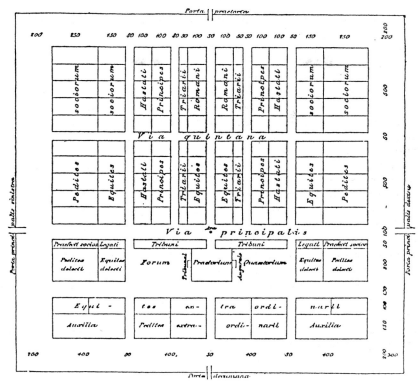

Fig. 5: Layout of a Roman military camp, according to Polybius.

become increasingly clear. The Sullan veteran colony of Allifae in central
Italy assumes the 'playing card' shape common in Roman forts. Many
Caesarian and Augustan settlements, of which Augusta Praetoria (Aosta)
is but one example (fig. 6), confirm the importance of the army in colonial
planning, and almost two hundred years later the same military influences
are still clearly apparent in the legionary colony of Thamugadi (Timgad)
in north Africa.

The other major factor in the development of this typically Roman grid
layout is land surveying. It is rarely possible in the ancient world to draw a
clear distinction between town and country. In the majority of cases town
dwellers were rural landowners and farm workers who lived in the cities but
went out to their fields every day to work. Conversely the rural population
were citizens of the local town and exercised their rights there. Thus the

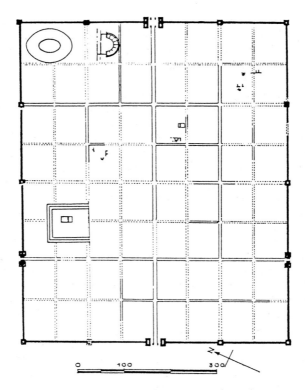

Fig. 6: Plan of the military colony of Augusta Praetoria (Aosta).

relationship between town and country was close. This is certainly true in Rome's colonies. Although the colonies were planted for military security, an essential part of the establishment, often to the detriment of the local population, was the confiscation and distribution of land to the colonists.[12] Land surveying was an integral feature of the establishment of the colonies. It seems natural therefore that the techniques of the land surveyors would be employed not only in distributing urban plots to the colonists but also in laying out the original town plan. Roman town planning therefore, although founded on established Graeco-Etruscan traditions, was the product of the specific needs of Roman colonisation. The experience which Rome gained in Italy laid the basis for Roman planning throughout the empire.

In conquering the European provinces in particular Rome was confronted with problems of security similar to those she had already met in Italy but on a much larger scale. In addition the city was to be the means of pacification and administration. But first of all urban centres had to be established and so the Roman concept of the city was transferred wholesale to the unurbanised parts of the empire. This resulted in the appearance throughout the western provinces of Romanised towns with fora, basilicae, bath houses, amphitheatres and the other trappings of Roman urban life. Moreover it was not only Rome's concept of the physical city that was transferred. Local administration closely followed the Roman pattern. There were annually elected magistrates similar to those at Rome and a permanent town council, drawn from the aristocracy and similar to the Senate.[13] In laying out these new towns the military surveyor and the engineer continued to play a major part and the town plans reflect the experience which Rome had already acquired in Italy.

We begin with Britain where, before the arrival of the Romans, there were effectively no towns. The Romans introduced regular planning and encouraged, sometimes with official assistance, Roman buildings and Roman constructional techniques.[14] Verulamium is typical of Roman planning efforts in Britain. The new town situated at the point where Watling Street crossed the River Ver replaced an earlier native centre. Its plan dates back to the Julio-Claudian period and developed as a series of approximately square *insulae* which were framed by rectilinear streets (fig. 7). The forum, the basilica of which was dedicated by Agricola,[15] lay close to one of the bridges across the river at the junction of two roads which led respectively northwards and westwards out of the town. Unlike the majority of the fora of British towns which were simple in design and probably derived from the headquarters building (*principia*) of a fort, the forum at Verulamium is more elaborate. The precinct itself is approximately square and is surrounded on three sides by colonnades under which were shops or offices, and on the fourth side by the Agricolan basilica.

As the town developed so more buildings were added. A masonry market building appeared towards the end of the first century A.D. as well as Romano-Celtic temples. After a devastating fire, one of several that Verulamium suffered, the forum was rebuilt in the reign of Antoninus Pius and a theatre was added. The town of Verulamium is Roman both in design and constructional techniques. Nevertheless the plan was adapted to the particular geographical circumstances of the site. The central intersection of the two main roads was abandoned and despite the regularity of the street plan, an oblique stretch of Watling Street was incorporated and entered the city through the southern gate.

The original Julio-Claudian town was defended by a ditch and bank rampart, although these defences proved inadequate during the revolt of

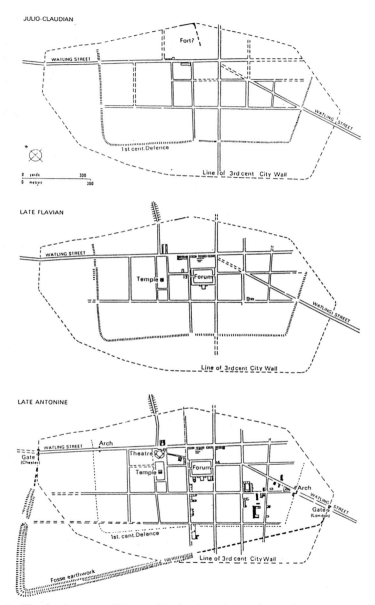

Fig. 7: The development of Roman Verulamium, first and second centuries A.D.

Boudicca when the town was destroyed. A new, more ambitious defensive scheme was initiated towards the end of the second century A.D. encompassing a far greater area. Stone-built gates and towers were erected as the first stage of the scheme. But as it turned out earth defences had to be constructed. The total area covered by the second-century city obviously proved to be too ambitious and when stone fortification walls were constructed in the third century A.D. the area of the city was again reduced in size.

Verulamium achieved the status of a *municipium*. Four colonies were also eventually developed at old legionary forts, and other towns were officially encouraged as *civitas* capitals. All these towns varied in size and detailed arrangements, as a comparison between places such as Venta Silurum (Caerwent) and Calleva (Silchester) reveals, but the underlying design was the same. Other towns grew spontaneously at forts, river crossings, road junctions and other strategic places.

The towns of Britain illustrate the ways in which Rome encouraged town life in an unurbanised province. In parts of Gaul the process of urbanisation was already more advanced because the Romans had been involved in Gaul for a longer period, and thus the towns were more developed. Sometimes the Romans moved existing Gallic *oppida* to new sites. Thus the Aeduan capital of Bibracte was replaced by the new Roman town of Augustodunum (Autun) in 5 B.C. On the other hand if a native centre was suitable a new town was developed at the existing site. Nemausus (Nîmes) and Arelate (Arles) are but two examples of pre-existing centres which were changed into fully Romanised native towns; likewise Augusta Treverorum (Trier), on the banks of the River Moselle, developed out of an existing native centre to become not only the tribal capital of the Treveri but also the capital of the breakaway 'empire of the Gauls', and under Diocletian's reorganisation of the empire the capital of the western provinces. Its role and importance as an urban centre was recognised as early as the reign of Claudius when it received the rank of *colonia*. Augusta Treverorum was laid out orthogonally along two intersecting arterial roads with the town's forum at the centre (fig. 8). Later the *decumanus maximus* was shifted to the south as the town expanded. Even so subsequent extensions to the town respected the original layout. As the town grew, so typical Roman urban buildings were added. An amphitheatre was built along the same axis as the forum on the eastern side of the city and it acted as one of the gates when the city was fortified. The forum itself, as in many towns, was perfectly fitted into the grid and occupied an area the equivalent of four *insulae*. In the second century A.D. the luxurious baths of St. Barbara were constructed close to the River Moselle and they were complemented by another

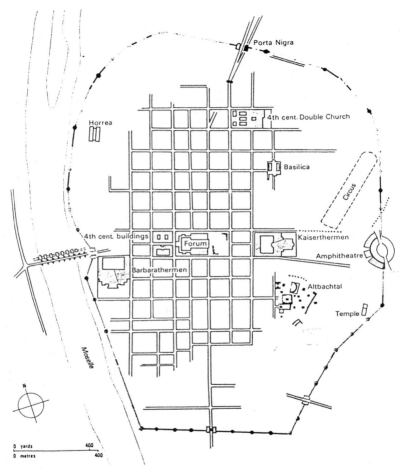

Fig. 8: Plan of Augusta Treverorum (Trier).

large bathing establishment in the reign of Constantine. When the town became an imperial capital a large palace was also constructed. Despite its Romanised appearance Augusta Treverorum remained an important religious centre of the Treveri. Consequently the town plan incorporated the existing religious district. It lay to the south of the baths of Constantine and contained many temples dedicated to native Celtic deities (cf. p. 87).

Within the regular framework of these native towns, typical Roman buildings and other urban facilities were developed. Fora more elaborate than those in Britain, basilicae, baths and amphitheatres became common features. Some towns even built theatres and circuses. Urban defences, the construction of which the central government was loath to sanction, were in the majority of cases not required because of the reality of the *Pax Romana*. Some of the towns of Gaul in particular display Roman technical achievements in the field of hydraulic engineering. Water was brought often great distances by means of aqueducts, to be distributed to fountains and buildings thoughout the city. Complementary to this is the provision of adequate drainage and sewerage facilities to carry off waste. In founding new towns the Romans used familiar techniques and tried methods. Yet the resulting cities themselves are not identical. Each is the product of its own particular local circumstance and is adapted to the immediate geographical and historical factors. The grid plan was established at the foundation of the town and controlled future developments, but the actual physical development of the town progressed slowly at a rate which was acceptable to the local population and according to the availability of finance.

Rome's achievement in fostering urban life in the unurbanised provinces of the empire is remarkable. Her problems were different in those parts of north Africa and the Greek East where cities already existed. Although new cities and colonies continued to be planted wherever the need or the opportunity arose, Rome's success in the urbanised parts of the empire was the way in which the existing cities were transformed. The Romans built upon established traditions, but they also introduced new ideas, new techniques and different constructional materials. The Roman love of axiality and symmetry, concepts which were only infrequently found in Hellenistic Greek planning, were popularised throughout the eastern provinces. Individual buildings, groups of buildings and even whole town plans were arranged along a central axis, promoting order and creating a balanced symmetrical arrangement. Together with this axial arrangement Roman concepts of monumentality, specifically Roman building types, colonnaded streets and lavish decoration were grafted on to existing cities. The result was fully Romanised provincial towns of diverse character and often spectacular appearance.

The variety of Roman achievements can first be witnessed in the Roman colonies and native towns of Africa. Northern Africa was crucial to Rome not only because of its grain, but also because of the rich trade from across the Sahara which brought to Rome luxury goods, exotic animals and slaves. As a result of Roman occupation, Roman colonies and Romanised native towns flourished during the imperial period. Comparison of the two Roman colonies of Thamugadi (Timgad) and Cuicul (Djemila)

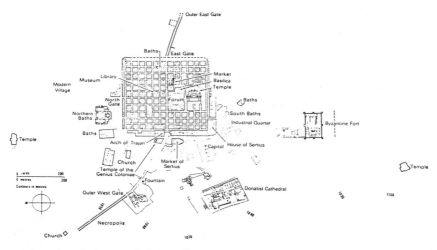

Fig. 9: Plan of Thamugadi (Timgad).

illustrates the adaptability of Roman techniques. The former represents Roman planning at its simplest. Thamugadi was planted early in the reign of the emperor Trajan as a veteran settlement for the troops of the legionary fort at Lambaesis. The layout is stark and military (fig. 9). Its perimeter is square with the rounded corners reminiscent of a fort. Two colonnaded streets lead from the three main gates of the town set in the northern, eastern and western walls to meet in the centre of the city where the forum is situated. Except for the area of the forum and the theatre, the rest of the city is divided into small square *insulae* by a series of intersecting streets. The rigid geometrical arrangement inside the city can be contrasted with developments outside the gates. Here the orthogonal arrangement is totally abandoned and the buildings developed without any order at all.

The stark military layout of the plan is relieved by the fine, decorated public buildings which catered for all aspects of Romanised urban life. The main streets were colonnaded, an increasingly common practice in many of the towns of the Greek East. Adjacent to the forum and its associated buildings was a theatre with a capacity for 3,500 to 4,000 people, and an ornate public latrine. There was also a public library, several temples and no less than twelve public bath houses, which is an indication of the importance of this type of building as a social institution of Roman cities.

The almost contemporary colony of Cuicul, established on a high precipitous hill in the mountainous hinterland of Algeria, has none of the

Fig. 10: Plan of Cuicul (Djemila).

rigidity of Thamugadi. The city was laid out in response to its location. The plan is regular but not rigidly so (fig. 10). The main axial north-south road is not perfectly straight, nor are all the lesser streets. The forum separates the original city from a later southwards extension. When the latter was added it was expertly incorporated into the existing city without the same incongruity as is apparent between the intra-mural and extra-mural occupation at Thamugadi.

Thamugadi and Cuicul were conceived as Roman cities; native cities were also Romanised to varying degrees. At Thugga (Dougga) a Romanised civic centre with forum, temples and market was constructed within the existing native town with its winding streets and cramped, bazaar-like domestic quarters. At Sabratha new public buildings and residential quarters were added to the original native harbour town. The native character of the new residential quarters was however maintained, and the new houses, shops and streets imitated the old harbour quarter in construction and style, although they tended to be more regular.

Lepcis Magna is probably the most impressive of the Romanised towns of Africa. The successive enlargements of the city carried out in the course of the first and second centuries A.D. and culminating with the extensive renovations of Septimius Severus completely transformed the original Punic town. The site was chosen by the Phoenicians in the sixth century B.C. to exploit one of the few natural harbours along the Tripolitanian coast. Under Augustus and his successors Lepcis flourished, far outgrowing the original town. The expansion however was rapid and unco-ordinated (fig. 11). A series of differently aligned rectangular extensions was added to the city along the line of the old road which curves gently to the southwest to lead to the rich olive producing districts of the south. As the town increased

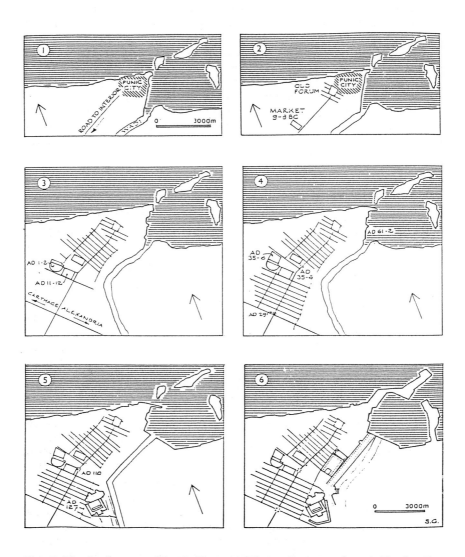

Fig. 11: The development of Lepcis Magna. 1. The pre-Roman nucleus; 2. The first Roman city; 3. The Augustan city (after 8 B.C.); 4. Julio-Claudian period (A.D. 14–68); 5. Under Trajan and Hadrian (early second century A.D.); 6. The Severan city (early third century A.D.).

in size new public buildings were added. The old forum with its temples and basilica linked the new extensions to the old harbour quarter. In 9/8 B.C. a new market was constructed on the then outskirts of the town; and a decade later the theatre was added. Lepcis continued to expand southwards towards the cross roads where the north-south axial road of the town met the main arterial road from Alexandria to Carthage. In the reign of Septimius Severus the junction was marked by a magnificent triumphal arch. Hadrian dedicated a large bath house on the south side of the city next to the Wadi Lebda, and in the third century A.D. the 'hunting baths' (cf. p. 62) were constructed in the western extension of the city along the coast.

Lepcis' greatest period of prosperity came under the reign of Septimius Severus (pl. 2). He sponsored an extensive programme of rebuilding which not only greatly embellished the city but also skilfully co-ordinated the disparate elements of the city. The basis of the new town was a large, lavishly decorated colonnaded street. Its raised porticoes were built of Karystos marble and the columns supported arches, not the usual architraves. It ran for 366 metres from the new enclosed harbour to pass behind the baths of Hadrian. Where the road bends at the baths of Hadrian an ornate *nymphaeum* (fountain house) was built. A new richly decorated forum and basilica was also added alongside the street. It was so constructed as to minimise the awkwardness of the site and to assist the unification of the different public elements of the city.

Because of the efforts of successive emperors Lepcis Magna far outgrew its Punic forerunner. Its buildings are grandiose, but nevertheless they retained Punic decorative details. The grandiosity of Lepcis Magna in part was due to the special interest of the emperor Septimius, who was born there. However, Lepcis reflects the changes which took place throughout the cities of the East under imperial and local patronage. One of the factors instrumental in the transformation of the cities of the eastern provinces was the vast resources which were available.[16] The cities benefited greatly from the gifts and benefactions of wealthy patrons, not only local citizens but also leading Roman figures and even the emperors themselves. Another factor was the established Hellenistic architectural traditions. The conquest of the East by Alexander and his successors had fused Greek and oriental traditions, and Rome built upon and expanded this combined tradition. Architecturally imposing buildings and groups of buildings, elaborate decoration even of the most utilitarian structures, and the use of height and bulk to impress and overawe were the hallmarks of the cities in the East. Even the old cities of Greece were not untouched. Corinth was rebuilt. The agora of Athens was remodelled. Indeed Athens was favoured by several wealthy patrons. Marcus Agrippa dedicated an odeion in the agora; Herodes Atticus dedicated a theatre. The emperor Hadrian took particular interest in the city. Under his patronage water supply was improved with the construction of a new aqueduct and a large holding tank at the foot of Lycabettus, whence it was distributed throughout the city. A new residential quarter was built and its boundary marked by a triple-gated triumphal arch; and the Temple of Olympian Zeus was finally completed. The great cities of Asia Minor were similarly treated. Miletos, Pergamon, probably the finest example of Hellenistic planning, and many other cities along the eastern coast of the Aegean were renovated and modernised. New buildings were added and urban facilities such as streets, drainage and water supplies were improved.[17]

Similar changes and renovations are noticeable throughout the cities of Asia Minor as Rome planted colonies and remodelled existing native towns. Aspendos, Side and Perge on Turkey's southern shore are only three of many existing towns which were greatly embellished in the Roman imperial period. The town plan of Perge is dominated by two arterial streets which intersect at right angles close to the acropolis, although the streets themselves are not perfectly rectilinear. These two streets were embellished, probably in the reign of Hadrian, by the addition of colonnades and a central stone built water channel which created two carriageways (pl. 3). The north-south road was particularly embellished. The inner courtyard of the earlier Hellenistic gate through which it passed was decorated with statues. Outside the earlier gate a large court was created, with a stoa, a monumental gateway, a monumental nymphaeum with a two-storeyed facade and a propylon. At the northern end of the colonnaded street there was a second nymphaeum with the usual water basin and a colonnade of Corinthian columns along the enclosing back wall. A large square agora was situated immediately to the east of the colonnaded street. Other public facilities included bath houses, a Graeco-Roman theatre, and a large stadium.

The area of direct Roman control stretched to the Euphrates. Throughout this region, much of it desert, the cities, which the Hellenistic kings and the Seleucids in particular had already established for military and political control, especially benefited from Rome's intervention, and under Roman control many of them reached their greatest extent. Unfortunately often it is not possible to study them in detail as they lie under modern cities.

Gerasa (Jerash) in the Jordanian desert, however, provides one example of the changes which were brought about by the Romans (fig. 12). The topography of the city was conditioned by the river Chrysorhoas which flows through the site and divides the city into two unequal parts. An arterial road running between the main northern and southern gate of the city lay

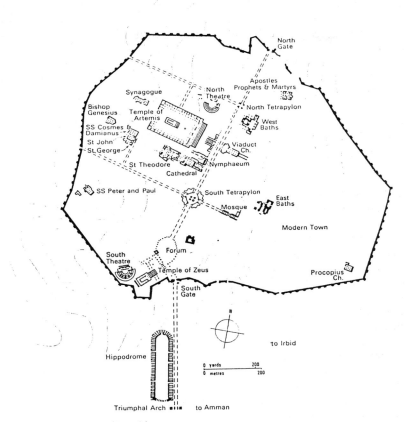

Fig. 12: Plan of Gerasa (Jerash).

on the western side of the Chrysorhoas ravine, and two other main roads at right angles to this route were carried across the river on bridges. A triumphal arch marked the intersection of the southernmost of these roads with the main north-south route. The three main streets and several of the lesser streets were colonnaded (pl. 4). At the southern end of the town the rectangular grid was abandoned. The southern gate leads obliquely on to an oval plaza, which forms the end of the arterial north-south road. In association with the plaza is one of the city's two theatres and a temple, dedicated to Zeus, but built in Romano-Syrian tradition and set upon a high podium. Further along the main road there was an ornate nymphaeum and propylaea which gave access to the precinct of the Temple of Artemis, one of the major religious monuments in the Roman East. Access to the precinct was by means of a monumental stairway, and the temple itself stood upon a high podium. There was a second theatre to the north of the precinct and there were also two baths.

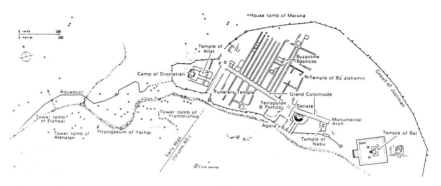

Fig. 13: Plan of Palmyra.

As one moves further east in this vast desert region the Roman way of life was maintained in the cities which acted as staging posts on the long distance trade routes to the Parthian empire. Palmyra is one such city. It flourished from the end of the Hellenistic period until the troubles which beset the empire in the third century A.D. The prosperity of the city rested on trade, both internal and through control of the long distance trade routes across its territory. The town plan was not totally homogeneous but the wide axial road running through the town gave a certain amount of unity and also linked the majority of the public buildings (fig. 13). The axial road itself was sumptuously colonnaded, the columns of which were adorned with statuary, a common feature in several cities of the East, although now only the fixing brackets remain. The street runs by means of three differently aligned sections from the great temple of Bel at its south eastern end to the funerary temple to the north west. The two changes in direction of the street are marked respectively by an elaborately decorated arch and a tetrapylon. The public buildings along the course of the street, including the Temple of Nebo, a theatre, the baths of Diocletian, an agora and a nymphaeum are also highly decorated. The Temple of Bel set in a large precinct dominates the eastern end of the city. The large square enclosure is artificially raised and is approached by means of a monumental stairway and surrounded internally by a colonnade of Corinthian columns. The temple itself, of typical Syrian plan, stood in the centre of the court. The Temple of Nebo was similarly set upon a high podium within a porticoed temenos in Corinthian style although the scale was different. The third major temple was dedicated to Ba'al Shamin and stands in a complex of courtyards. It was not only the public monuments which were lavish. Many of the private houses are equally grand and sumptuous, managing successfully to combine Hellenistic traditions and native Syrian elements.

The success of Roman planning in the East was founded upon established eastern traditions. Rome built on these traditions and added her own ideas. This combination of classical and oriental tradition not only transformed the cities of the Greek East but equally produced some of the most magnificent cities of the empire.

The history of Roman planning is rooted in practical experience. Rome developed a standard method of planning to deal with the recurring problems she faced throughout the empire in establishing cities and encouraging urban life. Although the approach was standard the resulting towns were not. Each is the result of its own particular geographical and historical circumstances. Local architectural traditions were included within the overall Roman framework. Although Roman planning was built upon the achievements of the Greeks and the Etruscans, the Romans were not mere imitators. They made their own independent contribution to the history of urban planning in the overall design of cities, in the construction and design of individual buildings, and in technological innovations which improved the quality of urban life. Town planning controlled future growth and formed the framework within which individual urban buildings developed. The latter form the basis of discussion of the subsequent chapters.

NOTES

1. Thucydides 2.4; Aristotle, *Politics* 1330b; Plutarch, *Pyrrhus* 32-34; Tacitus, *Annals* 15.38; 43 give some idea of the advantages and disadvantages.

2. Cicero, *de lege agraria* 2.96.

3. Thucydides 1.5; 10.

4. E.g. Poseidonia above, where the orientation of the temples differs from that of the streets; and Naples, where the original colony became a distinct and separate suburb after the construction of the new town.

5. Strabo, 5.3.8.

6. Servius on *Aeneid* 1.422.

7. Vitruvius, 1.7.1.

8. The original excavation report identified the north-west building as a temple, but it was subsequently suggested that it might have been a granary, see F. E. Brown, *Cosa: the making of a Roman town* (1980), 22.

9. J.B. Ward-Perkins, *Cities of Ancient Greece and Italy* (1974), 27f.

10. Frontinus, *Stratagems*, 4.1.14.

11. Polybius, 4.31.10.

12. E.g. the confiscations of the Sullan period, Cicero, *ad familiares* 13.4.1f; *ad Atticum* 1.19.4; *De domo sua* 79; the attitude of the colonists at Camulodunum was one of the reasons for the support which Boudicca received from the Trinovantes, Tacitus, *Annals* 14.31 (cf. also p. 86).

13. Tacitus, *Annals* 11.19; see also the charters of the Spanish towns of Salpensa and Malaca, ILS 6088-9, translated in Lewis and Reinhold, *Roman Civilization* II.320-6.

14. Tacitus, *Agricola* 21.

15. LACTOR, 4.26; S. Frere, *Britannia*[3] (1987), 191.

16. See Pliny, *Letters* 10.23 and 24; 38-40.

17. See the case of Amastris' drainage, Pliny, *Letters* 10.98.

2. Civic and Other Buildings

John Carter

Temples, water supply, and places for entertainment—which are given separate treatment in later chapters of this book—were all striking or important features of ancient cities. But there was a great deal else that a city needed before it could claim to possess the dignity and facilities that enabled it to function as the largely independent civic unit which in practice it was. The towns of Italy and the Roman provinces may have been under the control of Rome, but in most respects they continued to arrange and administer their own affairs in the tradition of the self-governing city-states which had been the creation of the Greeks several centuries before. They therefore required buildings where political and administrative activity could take place, where health and recreation could be attended to, and where the trade and business that characterised any urban centre could be conducted.

The physical planning of towns was discussed in the previous chapter, but it is beyond question that the general character and 'feel' of the ordinary Graeco-Roman town of the empire were strongly influenced by the architectural ideas that had become the norm in the Greek world before the coming of Rome. These ideas had themselves been conditioned by social customs and expectations and by judgments about the value of particular activities. One of the most important of these judgments, so far as the history of architecture is concerned, was that the proper mode of civilised existence was urban. The result was that when the community (or its benefactors) decided to build, the aim was always to improve the amenities of the urban centre and add to its impressiveness and civic status. Except in the case of certain religious sanctuaries which were distant from any urban centre and might be furnished with stoas, meeting-rooms and even theatres, such building almost invariably took place within the walls of the town. There also existed in this city-state culture an intense local patriotism and a desire to go one better than the neighbours. Thus every town with any pride or pretensions to importance gradually acquired a number of public buildings which make up a standard set.

What this set was we can glean not only from the remains themselves but also from the architectural treatise written by Vitruvius. When in Book 5 he sets out 'the arrangement of public places' (*publicorum locorum dispositiones*) he lists almost exactly the buildings that were to be found in any Greek city: forum and basilica; treasury, prison, and council-house; theatre with adjoining porticoes; baths; palaestra; and harbours and shipyards. Both forum and theatre are specifically discussed by Vitruvius with reference to their differences from their Greek counterparts; nearly all the examples of porticoes attached to theatres are from the Greek world (indeed, they could hardly be otherwise at the time he wrote); baths are an institution which had spread to Roman culture from the Greek cities of Campania; the palaestra is specifically admitted by Vitruvius not to be a usual thing in Italy; and the space given to harbours and shipyards seems to reflect Greek rather than Italian priorities. Of the other buildings, treasury and prison, though necessary, are of minor importance and seem never to have been thought worthy of much attention, while council- or senate-houses are an expected feature in a world where the self-governing, or at least self-administering, community was the standard form of political life. The one building which stands out as a peculiarly Roman type is the basilica, a large covered hall which performed the function of the ubiquitous stoas of Hellenistic architecture and is obviously loosely related to them, but had a form which appears to lack any clear parallel in the Greek world.

The basilica went on to become, along with the great bath-buildings of the Empire, a major vehicle of Roman originality and development in architecture. In both cases we start with a Roman adaptation, or borrowing, of structures created by the Greeks, and end up with something impressively different and entirely Roman in scale and purpose. But at the time that Vitruvius wrote we are at the end of the period of two hundred years or so during which the tide of Hellenisation had flowed into central Italy as the Romans and their Italian allies became ever more powerful, and their cities, above all Rome itself, ever more receptive to Greek culture. If we supplement Vitruvius with a look at the actual remains of the public buildings of the Republican period, we can obtain a fair idea of the half-Greek, half-indigenous base from which the architecture of the Empire sprang.

I. Republican Italy

The physical remains that are known to us from central Italy provide an interesting commentary on Vitruvius and show very clearly that the development of the characteristic urban centre of imperial times was already well advanced by the early first century B.C. This archaeological evidence confirms Vitruvius' general picture, while adding some types of building not mentioned by him. These seem to be either of an unglamorous and sternly practical nature, like granaries and market-buildings, or else connected with an older Italic tradition independent of Hellenistic theory, like the *atria* and *comitium* known from Rome and now well exemplified at Cosa.

Cosa (Ansedonia), whose foundation in 273 B.C. was described in chapter 1 (p. 12), acquired in the course of the next one hundred and fifty years all the public buildings that a flourishing small town of the time needed—first, high on its sloping site, its chief temples, then lower down, clustering around its forum, two more temples, a basilica, a senate-house (*curia*) with flanking offices and adjoining formal meeting-area (*comitium*), a prison modelled on that of Rome, and blocks of public rooms or shops (*atria*). In the second century porticoes were built along the north and west sides of the forum. They had widely spaced chunky columns very different from their elegant models in the stoas of the Hellenistic world. Porticoes were erected in other colonies[1] at the same time, and it is evident that we are seeing the impact of the eastern Mediterranean on Italy: not only in literature and the fine arts did 'captive Greece take her fierce conqueror captive', as Horace's famous phrase has it.[2] These buildings are arranged in a loosely balanced way, but without any formal symmetry, around the open rectangle of the forum itself (pl. 5 shows the northern corner, with formal entrance in the middle of the north-western side, *atrium*, basilica with overlying theatre, circular *comitium*, and senate-house). The forum served not only as the chief square of the town, but also as the voting enclosure for the assembly of citizens when they met to elect magistrates or pass legislation. On its uphill (south-western) side is an enormous underground cistern, one of whose outlets fed two long water-troughs which suggest the existence, in a portico at the south-western entrance to the forum, of a market (*macellum*), particularly one for fish and meat. There is nothing certainly to identify the treasury (though it could have occupied one of the side chambers of the Curia). Of the other structures mentioned by Vitruvius, Cosa lacked a palaestra and (in common with all purely Roman towns before the first century B.C.) a theatre,[3] while baths, if any, will have been modest private establishments built relatively late in this period. Cosa, on its isolated hill beside the sea, must always have faced difficulty in securing adequate supplies of water for such 'luxury' purposes. There is also a most interesting artificial harbour, together with hydraulic control works which seemingly have to do with the farming of fish, but these lie outside the scope of the present discussion.[4]

The excavations of recent years at another colony, Alba Fucens, founded in 303 B.C. in the central Apennines between the now drained Fucine Lake and the mountains that close it in on the north, have revealed the same combination of forum, basilica, and *macellum* as at Cosa, though differently disposed. At Cosa, the basilica lies off-centre along one of the long sides of the forum. At Alba it occupies the whole of one end and is centred on the main (longitudinal) axis of the forum, from which it is separated by a feature unusual in this position, a narrow peristyle or colonnaded court (presumably to provide some shelter in the mountain weather). In both cases the length of the building is parallel to the side of the forum. At Alba the *macellum* lies directly behind the basilica, which screened it from the forum and did not allow direct passage from one to the other. The visible remains of the *macellum* are of a circular courtyard surrounded by a dozen wedge-shaped 'shops', fitted into a nearly square rectangle; but this is a rebuilding of the late first or early second century A.D. adopting a form that was fashionable at the time in this area of Italy.[5] The underlying Republican structure, of c.150–100 B.C., leaves the rectangle largely open, with small open-fronted spaces for the stall-holders created by a number of short walls running in from the perimeter wall. There is a large cistern for the water essential for washing and sluicing, and a well-designed drainage system to carry it away.

Pompeii, unlike Cosa and Alba Fucens, was an old and flourishing town when in 80 B.C. the Roman government, to punish the inhabitants for having backed the wrong side in the civil wars which had just been concluded, established a colony of veteran soldiers there. The native community were Oscan-speaking Campanians of central Italic origin, who had infiltrated and absorbed the Greek settlements which had been established around the Bay of Naples between the eighth and the sixth centuries. Their hybrid culture had something of the Italic and something of the Greek in it. In the third and second centuries they shared in the prosperity that came to the whole area as a result of the overseas expansion of Roman power and the enormous accompanying increase in trade between the Aegean world and Italy. Thus Pompeii, whose foundation goes back to at least the sixth century B.C., already possessed before the end of the second century all

the buildings mentioned by Vitruvius. These include the very Greek insti-
tutions of theatre and palaestra, and also two sets of baths and the oldest
basilica of which more than the traces can be seen.

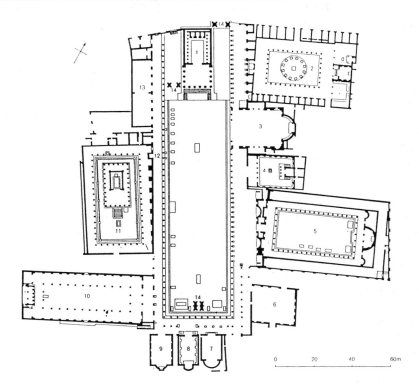

Fig. 14: Plan of the Forum, Pompeii. 1. Temple of Jupiter; 2. Provision market (*macellum*); 3. Sanctuary of the City Lares; 4. Temple of Vespasian; 5. Cloth
traders' hall (Eumachia building); 6. Voting hall (*comitium*); 7. Chief magistrates' (duovirs') office; 8. Council chamber (*curia*); 9. Junior magistrates'
(aediles') office; 10. Basilica; 11. Temple of Apollo; 12. Control of weights and
measures; 13. Cereals market; 14. Commemorative arches.

The layout of the forum is very Italic (fig. 14), dominated at one end
by the axially placed Temple of Jupiter (whose foundation precedes the
arrival of the Romans) and at the other by a trio of municipal offices,
including the senate-house. Macellum and basilica open on to it, placed
asymmetrically and unobtrusively in corners, while tucked away behind
one side is the colonnaded precinct which contains the fifth-century temple

of Apollo. The comitium, a small quadrilateral, occupies a third corner, and in the fourth, beside the Temple of Jupiter, is the vegetable market. This latter is basically a development of a line of shops (*tabernae*) such as survived at Rome itself incorporated into the grandiose buildings of the late republican forum. Pompeii offers an excellent example of how the old irregular market-place of an Italian town could be transformed by the existing native predisposition towards axiality and by the strong influences from Hellenistic Greek architecture to produce a dignified centre that was still a hub of everyday life. A notable feature of the forum of Pompeii was the two-storeyed stone porticoes, built in the second century, which surrounded it on three sides in imitation of the stoas and colonnades which were to be found in a contemporary Hellenistic city.

Rather different from any of the foregoing is the hill-town of Aletrium (Alatri), which lies above the valley of the Trerus on the line of the Via Latina, the ancient inland route from Rome southwards. It was neither planned afresh, like Cosa or Alba, nor occupied a level site, like Pompeii, but in the second century its inhabitants were prosperous enough to create on the site of their citadel (*arx*) at the top of the town a great terraced platform with enormously impressive walls and access ramps. Otherwise, not a great deal remains to be seen. However, there survives an inscription[6] from the late second century B.C. commemorating one of the leading citizens, L. Betulienus Varus. With the approval of the local senate, Varus saw to the making of the following: 'all the paths in the town, the entrance portico to the *arx*, the sports field, the clock, the *macellum*, the stuccoing of the basilica, seats, a water-tank for the baths, a water-tank by the gate, and the construction of a water-supply to the town to a height of 340 feet with arches and solid[7] pipes'. It is not clear whether Varus paid for any of this himself. Analogies from elsewhere make it likely that he did, but no matter. The inscription stands as vivid evidence for the dramatic improvements in urban facilities that were occurring in the towns of Italy as a result of the growth of Rome as an imperial power. These changes are nowhere more apparent or more influential than at Rome itself, and it is time to turn to the capital. What is the relationship of its architecture, in the first place to that of the smaller and more ordinary places we have so far been considering, and secondly to those currents of Hellenisation which had since the third century been flowing ever more powerfully towards central Italy?

II. Republican Rome

The most important single process in the development of Roman architecture is the gradual adoption of concrete as a constructional material. It was this, with its great strength and versatility, which made possible the huge vaulted interiors of the imperial baths and the domes and curves of lesser structures—all forms which were fundamentally antipathetic to the vocabulary of Greek architecture inherited by the Romans, and had nothing to do with the logic of post-and-lintel construction. The arch had indeed been used by the Greeks from about the time of Alexander, but seldom in other than subterranean or supporting structures, safely out of sight. When it did appear (as for example over one of the gates of Priene) it was ostentatiously emphatic and remained unmarried to more traditional architectural forms. The Romans and Etruscans, on the other hand, had a natural competence as structural engineers, revealed in their ability to terrace and to build complex water supply and drainage systems, and they readily adopted the arch at a time when their own architectural style was relatively primitive and much less set than that of Greece.

The volcanic areas of the Tyrrhenian side of Central Italy are short of high-quality building stone, but rich in deposits of sands which make an extremely durable mortar (including a variety capable of setting under water).[8] Thus it was possible to substitute for cut-stone construction a mass of rubble bonded into a solid substance with this mortar and faced by setting the better pieces of stone at the outside. Such was the strength of the mortar that builders came to realise that they could use quite small pieces, only two or three inches across, for facing, while the rubble aggregate behind could be composed of almost any size of stone that came to hand. This stage had been reached in Campania before the end of the third century B.C., but the further refinement of the technique, in conjunction with arched or vaulted structures, seems to have taken place in Rome and Latium.

It has recently been argued that the magnificent terrace on which stands the temple of Jupiter Anxur at Terracina was built late in the third century to guard the coast road against Hannibal.[9] If this is so, the next hundred years or so saw little or no development. The concrete arcading which supports the terrace already exploits the constructional possibilities of the new material by using it to create forms hitherto the province of cut stone, and the facing in small, irregular, stones set in the random manner known as *opus incertum* is indistinguishable from the work of c. 100 B.C., to which date the terrace is usually assigned. The earliest datable concrete in Rome itself is in the substructures of the temple of Magna Mater on the Palatine, which was dedicated in 191 B.C.[10] More spectacular is the noble ruin of the Porticus Aemilia, a huge warehouse near the Tiber consisting of fifty barrel-vaulted bays divided from each other by arcades of seven arches whose tops do not reach the spring of the barrel-vault (fig. 15). Thus there is no groining. The whole structure is in concrete faced with *opus incer-*

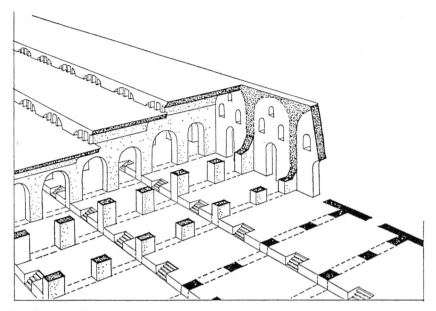

Fig. 15: Rome, Porticus Aemilia: axonometric plan.

tum. The only sign of any lack of confidence on the part of the engineers of this massive structure is that at the end of each bay they offset the upper windows from the lower, so that the perforations in the wall slab are evenly distributed over its surface and create the minimum of structural weakness.

The building has been dated to 174 B.C. on the basis of a note in Livy (41.40) which records it as a reconstruction of a previous *porticus* and details other building activity on the part of the censors of that year. This note forms part of a series of scattered items of information which make it quite clear that both the centre of the city and the Tiber-side port were being enormously developed in the first quarter of the century. On the other hand it is slightly odd that (if one excepts the Terracina terrace, which is in any case considerably simpler) no structure of anything like the same degree of size and technical mastery survives from the next fifty years— and this at a time when the city of Rome was growing richer, bigger, and more cosmopolitan by the minute. It is perfectly possible that the Porticus Aemilia we see (whose identification is secured by the fragments of the Severan marble plan of the city) is another rebuilding carried out in the third or last quarter of the century, perhaps in connection with the state-run system of grain supply to the capital introduced by Gaius Gracchus in 123 B.C., perhaps simply to meet the needs of a market that had to cater for an expanding population already numbered in hundreds of thousands.[11]

Whatever the date of the Porticus Aemilia, it is evident that it belongs to that development of the port of Rome, downstream of the island in the Tiber, and near to the vegetable and cattle markets, which brought with it the construction of other warehouses, granaries, and market buildings. The physical evidence has almost entirely disappeared, but the literary evidence along with the Severan plan leaves us in no doubt that the Romans erected a number of utilitarian buildings in this area. We know of two granaries (*horrea*) here: one the Semproniana or Gracchana, which was certainly due to C.Gracchus, the other the Galbana. It is highly probable that such buildings provided the opportunity for architects, engineers and builders to gain confidence in the use of concrete and to discover its potentialities and its limitations. The Horrea Galbana of c.100 B.C., if correctly identified with the building of warehouse type with three great courtyards lying immediately behind the Porticus Aemilia, has yielded the earliest certain example of the next development of Roman concrete—that is, the substitution of a perfectly regular facing, giving a diagonal net pattern (*opus reticulatum*), in place of the earlier irregular (*incertum*) or semi-regular (*quasi-reticulatum*) facings. Vitruvius is suspicious of the technique,[12] observing that cracks are more likely to occur along the straight joint lines. He was in fact wrong, because the strength of the structure lies in the concrete core and not in the facing, as the ruins of many a Roman building testify. It is, none the less, not obvious why a method of construction that required more care and gave no improvement in strength was adopted, especially as a coating of plaster, which hid the neat pattern, was commonly applied. The explanation may well be that advanced by Coarelli: what we are witnessing is the adoption of industrial methods of building, stimulated by the demand generated by the booming Roman economy and suited to execution by a slave labour force.[13] Given a situation where the demand is such that facing stones have to be cut, rather than just picked up, it is no more trouble to produce regular than irregular shapes, and standardisation will enable low-grade (or at least poorly motivated) workers to increase their output. The availability of standard units will also speed up the routine of building walls.

Part of Vitruvius' distrust, not only of *opus reticulatum*, but of all concrete work of this Roman type which lacked through-bonding, arises from his refusal to believe that the mortar will not break down and lose its strength over a number of years. He tells us, presumably correctly, that the valuers of his day deducted one-eighteenth of the cost of these walls for every year of their age, whereas walls of unbaked brick were valued at cost irrespective of age.[14] The inference must be that it took a long period of experiment in the second and early first centuries before Roman builders fully mastered the various strengths and types of 'mix' that were required in different circumstances and by different combinations of materials. But in spite of such conservative misgivings, concrete had left behind its utilitarian origins before the end of the second century, as the great terraced and arcaded hillside sanctuary of Fortuna at Praeneste proves (see pp. 73f). At Rome, we find concrete vaulting used in the galleries of the Tabularium, the public record office built by Q. Lutatius Catulus in the early seventies B.C. The platform and lower storey of this building still stand, with Renaissance upperworks, at the head of the Republican forum (pls. 6,7). It is typically Roman in at least three ways. It stands on a platform in just the way that country houses, large and small, were routinely beginning to do, in order to find a level base against a hillside and to acquire a certain impressiveness of aspect; it frames its arches in a structurally unnecessary but aesthetically satisfying manner, borrowing respectability in the shape of columns and entablature from the traditional vocabulary of Greek architecture; and although it does not have true groined vaults, it shows in the bays of its gallery the beginnings of that Roman engagement with vaulted and curved interior space which was to lead to the triumphs of Imperial architecture. The Tabularium is an interesting hybrid between a functional storage space and a piece of public architecture intended to adorn the forum and impress the world. We also happen to know that its architect was a man of Italian origin, who had served under Catulus as *praefectus fabrum* (colonel of engineers).[15]

Almost as important in the history of Roman architecture is the function performed by the capital in providing models for the 'little Romes' which the newly founded colonies like Cosa and Alba Fucens constituted. The most striking example is the complex of Curia (senate-house) and Comitium (ceremonial meeting-area). At Rome, the old Republican senate-house ascribed to King Tullus Hostilius, together with the Comitium which lay directly in front of it, formed a sacred inaugurated space (*templum*) aligned exactly north-south (cf. p. 82). By the late fourth or early third century the comitium had assumed the form of a circle within the rectangular field of the *templum*. It is this layout that we find repeated at Cosa, Alba Fucens, and Paestum, all colonies founded between 303 and 273. It is possible, given the existence in the south of Italy of circular Greek assembly-places of the sixth or fifth century, that the Romans borrowed the idea from the Greeks. But once adopted at Rome, it became the pattern for offshoots of Rome. The Roman Comitium has long since vanished, paved over when the growth of Rome had made its limited space an inadequate arena for political debate and decision. The Curia, however, is still with us (pls. 6,7). What we see is a rebuilding of the time of Diocletian of the Curia Julia, begun by Julius Caesar and completed by Augustus on a slightly different site from that of the Curia Hostilia (as rebuilt by Sulla), which had been burnt down at Clodius' impromptu funeral in the forum in 52 B.C.[16] It is a conservative building, conforming fairly well to the precepts given by Vitruvius for the proportions of a curia,[17] and having a timber roof. Its sole adornment was an elaborate porch (*chalcidicum*) which appears on the simplified but recognisable likeness found on coins of Augustus. Because of its venerable associations it is the sort of structure least likely to be the vehicle of innovation. But *curiae* were found all over the Roman world, an essential part of the civic scene and a reminder in every forum of the dignity and importance of the local senate.

To the right of the Curia Julia can be seen the remains of the Basilica Paulli. The original building on the site (179 B.C.) belongs to the trio of basilicas in the forum of Rome which are the earliest attested examples of the type, the others being the Porcia of 184 B.C. and the Sempronia of 169 B.C.[18] These large covered halls placed beside the main business and political centre of the city corresponded in function to the stoas of the Greek world, which were long open-fronted colonnades, universal in the civic centres of the Hellenistic period, sometimes having upper storeys and sometimes being deep enough to contain shops. The Roman version is essentially different, in that it has a true interior. (The fact that some basilicas had a colonnade open to the forum does not alter the validity of this observation.) The possession of an interior space of some size and impressiveness meant that the building could exist in and for itself and become a frame for activities and rituals (the giving of judgment, the veneration of the imperial family) to which the stoa was quite unsuited.

The origins of the basilica are obscure, in that no clear precursor from the eastern Mediterranean, where its Greek name would seem to locate it, has come to light. Precedents have been sought in Ptolemaic Alexandria and in the so-called 'hypostyle hall' on Delos, a large columned hall with a colonnaded front and a form of clerestory roof, but the match is not very good. A better approach may be to assume that the Italian peoples were in fact capable of inventing an architectural form in response to the demands of their climate and their social, legal and business life —the purposes which are expressly mentioned by Suetonius[19] when he gives Augustus' reasons for wishing to build another forum, of which a basilica is but a covered extension. An examination of the prehistory of the Basilica Paulli lends some support to this view. Plautus uses the term *subbasilicani* to mean 'men who hang around the basilica' in a play written before 200 B.C.[20] The basilica in question may well be the early one lying beneath the Basilica Paulli. It was probably built in 209 B.C. after a fire which swept the area the previous year [21] and destroyed the Atrium Regium (i.e. 'the *atrium* [hall] near the Regia'). 'Basilica' (the Greek translation of Regium) is then explained as an accident of local toponymy.[22] Why Greek? Perhaps it was a piece of cultural fashion, perhaps a genuine acknowledgement that the new public hall had moved a long way towards the Greek stoa from its previous traditionally Roman form—and one may see from Cosa how the indisputably Italic *atria* round the forum duplicated the heart of the Roman house and bore little resemblance to any public building of the Greek world. This is an attractive theory and has the additional merit of explaining why the Roman adaptation of the stoa is a hall.

Whatever its origins, the basilica spread rapidly. Cosa's appears to date from about the middle of the second century; those of Pompeii, Ardea and Alba straddle the end of the century, by which time Rome had a fourth, the Opimia. So far as they can be reconstructed, they were very similar to each other in form; the distinction between the 'long' type (entrance on the short side) or the 'broad' type (entrance on the long side) seems to have little significance. A rectangle of interior columns divided the space into a kind of surrounding aisle and a central area with a higher roof which acted as a lantern or clerestory and gave the necessary illumination. Vitruvius has left us a detailed description of the basilica he built at Fanum Fortunae (Fano) in northern Umbria.[23] Above its aisle there ran a gallery, supported on pilasters attached to the back of fifty-foot columns arranged, in plan, in an 8 x 4 formation (120 x 60 Roman feet); these ran right up to the central roof, which was some feet above the roof of the surrounding gallery. Thus a clerestory was created which admitted light and air to the interior of the building. Vitruvius' comment on the novelty of his giant columns makes it clear that the usual arrangement was indeed to include such a gallery, but to give each storey its own order and entablature, as in a two-storeyed stoa. The Fano basilica also had recessed into the middle of the (long) side opposite the forum an elaborate dais or tribunal, a feature found in varying arrangements in most of the others and still clearly visible at Pompeii (pl. 8). The roofs, both side and main, will presumably have been pitched and tiled, although at Cosa the excavators restore over the single-storey aisle a flat roof serving as an outdoor promenade.

At Rome, the Basilica Paulli, certainly in the form in which it was rebuilt in the first century B.C. by L. Aemilius Paullus and possibly originally, possessed all along its frontage on to the Sacra Via a two-storeyed portico which was deep enough to contain shops (the Tabernae Novae, 'New Shops'). Between the shops there were three entrances to the main hall of the basilica lying directly behind them. Above them, reached by a flight of stairs at either end, was a repetition of the arrangement, probably also with access into the basilica itself at the level of its internal gallery. It would have been a magnificent place from which to watch processions or the shows which were given in the forum. As befitted the status of the great political family of the Aemilii, it acquired in the course of its successive reconstructions great splendour of material and ornament. Some indication of the architectural effect can be gained from the drawing made by Sangallo in the late fifteenth century when more of the building was standing (pl. 9). A relief frieze of marble depicting the legend of Tarpeia survives, and there is evidence to suggest that the columns were also of marble, very probably of an exotic variety (Pliny says Phrygian): Paullus' father, M. Lepidus, who was consul in 78 B.C. and rebuilt the neighbouring Basilica Aemilia, is recorded as having an astonishingly luxurious private house and being the first Roman to use Numidian marble.[24] Perhaps more significant (since luxury became commonplace and Rome is where one would expect to find it) is the basilica's trapezoidal site, determined by two ancient roads or paths, and its lack of any clear axial relationship to other buildings or to a neatly defined public space. Rome was old, her public buildings and civic spaces bore no planned relationships to each other, and it took time before the regularity visible in her colonies found expression in the capital.

III. Augustan Rome

During the transformation of the state which began with Caesar and was complete in its essential aspects by the time of Augustus' death, architecture passed, at least in respect of great public buildings, from being a method of self-advertisement to an expression and instrument of political power. In Augustan Rome, the spectator was endlessly confronted with structures which bore the name or were associated with the deeds or family of the emperor. Altars, temples, arches, aqueducts, theatres, porticoes, baths, markets, fora, even the senate-house itself, proclaimed the vast scale of the provision which Augustus made for the people of Rome. The Roman aristocracy had long advertised themselves by commissioning buildings or monuments which bore their names, whether these were paid for by themselves or by the state on their initiative. The three early basilicas referred to above are a case in point. Such splendid gifts to the people were indicators of the effectiveness of the aristocracy as leaders and benefactors of the community. They laid a claim to the gratitude, and where appropriate the votes, of the ordinary man. The Roman elite were highly competitive. As the struggle for power intensified during the last fifty years of the Republic men coveted the opportunity to erect, or oversee the erection of, great public buildings. Q. Catulus, a prominent figure in the party of Sulla, secured for himself control not only of the construction of the Tabularium (see above), but also of the rebuilding of the Capitoline Temple, burnt in a fire in 83 B.C. His ideas for modernising the appearance and decoration of the archaic temple were so grandiose that the work was twenty years in the completion. So great was the competition for status and influence, and so great the rewards of success, that when Julius Caesar stood for the relatively unimportant (in themselves) offices of aedile and Pontifex Maximus, he thought it worth while laying out a sum of money huge enough for it to require the conquest of Gaul to retrieve his fortunes.

It is in this context that we need to place the great public benefactions of Pompey, in the shape of his theatre (see p. 101), and of Julius Caesar, in the shape of his Basilica, Curia and Forum. Both the Sullan Curia and the adjoining old Basilica Porcia had been burnt down in 52 B.C., so the project of replacing them was unremarkable, indeed necessary. But it seems characteristic of Caesar that he wished to make a huge improvement in the facilities and appearance of the somewhat haphazardly arranged forum of the city that ruled the Mediterranean world. All three projects were unfinished at his death and were completed by his heir Octavian (the future Augustus). The Curia has already been discussed above (p. 41). The Basilica stood on the west side of the Forum (fig. 16) where its plan is still visible, replacing the Tabernae Veteres ('Old Shops') and the second-century Basilica Sempronia. It was an enormous double-aisled building with colonnades open to the Forum on its north, east and south sides, and at the back shops at both ground and first-floor level. In plan and size it is simply an elaborated version of what was by now obviously a very standard type of building, but its construction is interesting. Instead of interior columns, there were piers carrying arches, and the roofs of aisles and galleries were vaulted. Evidently, the methods of utilitarian architecture were starting to invade grand civic buildings. The exterior was of marble, with the arcades framed, after the fashion of the neighbouring Tabularium arches, by engaged columns carrying a Tuscan entablature. Thus we have a significant combination of Roman structural techniques, Greek architectural articulation and imperial lavishness of material. The Basilica Julia is prophetic.

Equally significant, though it confirms rather than foretells, is the Forum Julium, Caesar's addition to the central public space of Rome. To create it, he bought up and demolished property lying behind and to the north of his Curia (fig. 17), and built a rectangular forum surrounded by porticoes on three sides. On the fourth (narrow) side was the Temple of Venus Genetrix, vowed on the battlefield of Pharsalus, which dominated

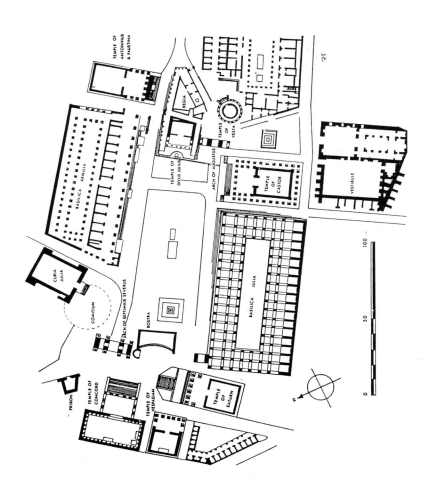

Fig. 16: Rome, Forum Romanum: plan.

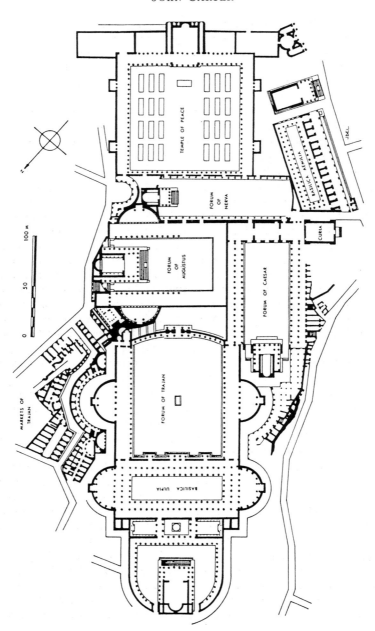

Fig. 17: Rome, Imperial Fora: plan.

the axis of the forum and was flanked by a pair of arches. At the back of the portico on the west side were shops constructed in cut stone (*opus quadratum*) with flat arches forming the lintels of the openings, though the barrel vaults within are believed not to be original but to date from the Flavian period. The whole ensemble is a product of the same architectural thought which shaped the forum of Pompeii, with its axially dominant temple at one end and its surrounding porticoes, and found expression in the positioning of the basilica of Alba Fucens centrally at the head of its forum. The surrounding marble-columned porticoes are of course Greek in inspiration, but the axial composition and the presence, however unobtrusive, of shops reflect even in this metropolitan piazza basic elements of Italic life.

The population of Rome for whom Caesar provided these splendid new buildings suffered from the civil wars and disturbances which characterised the years between Caesar's murder in 44 B.C. and Augustus' victory over Antony and Cleopatra at Actium in 31 B.C. But because their goodwill was politically important, they profited from building activity on the part of the great. In 33 B.C. Agrippa, Augustus' right-hand man, went so far as to assume the aedileship, an unprecedentedly humble office for an ex-consul, in order to carry out a comprehensive repair and maintenance programme on the water-supply and sewers of Rome. He also provided the people with free barbers and baths, and when the regime of Augustus was firmly established after 27 B.C. he continued to see that they were properly looked after. To this end he embarked on a great series of public works, many of them on the Campus Martius (cf. fig. 51), which became Rome's equivalent of London's Hyde Park and South Bank combined.[25]

Agrippa's Thermae are the first to bear that name, and the first of a long series of ever more palatial bath-buildings provided by the emperors for their people. Agrippa's are by the standards of the later examples very modest, but they indicate a decisive change in architectural tone. Hitherto public baths in Rome had been small affairs termed *balnea*, presumably of little architectural pretension (none survive), and definitely not places of much social respectability (as Cicero's *pro Caelio* reveals). Hot-air or steam baths were known in the Greek world in the fifth century B.C. and must have been established in Campania by the third century. Seneca speaks of the dark and cramped bath of the villa at Liternum of the great Scipio Africanus, who died in retirement there in 184 B.C.[26] Two sets of public baths of the Republican period are known from Pompeii, the Stabian and Forum Baths. The plan of the latter (fig. 18), which date from about 80 B.C., shows two suites of rooms (men's and women's) either side of a central furnace chamber, all fitted in to a typical Roman *insula* block with shops on two sides. There is also a small exercise courtyard (*palaestra*),

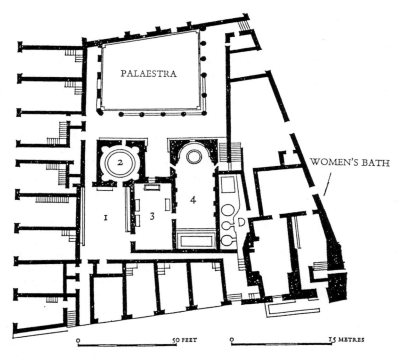

Fig. 18: Pompeii, Forum Baths: plan. 1. Dressing room (*apodyterium*); 2. Cold room (*frigidarium*); 3. Warm room (*tepidarium*); 4. Hot room (*caldarium*).

a typically Greek feature. The women's side is obviously inferior, but the men's side shows all the essential features of the Roman bath-building: at the left, the dressing room (*apodyterium*) gave access either to a circular domed cold room (*frigidarium*) containing a plunge bath or to a warm room (*tepidarium*) which led to the hot room (*caldarium*). This latter had a half-dome over one end and a plunge bath and basin. The heating was effected by drawing hot air from the furnace under the suspended tile floor to flues in the walls, a system alleged to have been invented, or at least substantially improved, by one C. Sergius Orata[27] in the early first century B.C. The Stabian Baths illustrate the arrangement, and also the concrete or rubble-work vaulting so well suited to withstand the heat and the steam of the baths.

    It is unlikely to be an accident that the earliest concrete domes of Roman architecture occur in Campania, where the natural conditions favoured the development of these thermal baths. The so-called 'Temple of Mercury' at Baiae, a domed hall almost half the diameter of the Pantheon, forms part of a bath complex which certainly belonged to one of the luxury seaside villas, perhaps the emperor's own, which clustered in this fashionable and desirable spot. It dates from the very late Republican or early Augustan period and thus is contemporary with Agrippa's Thermae in Rome, built in 25 B.C. The vault is of concrete only 60 cm thick with radially laid aggregate of tufa, the light volcanic stone. It has a central *oculus*, demonstrating that by this time Roman builders understood that once a concrete structure had hardened it ceased to be subject to dynamic internal stresses and it was only gravity which had to be taken into account. Thus in the case of a dome, perforations in the skin no more caused it to collapse than would holes of the same relative size made in half a tennis ball.

Agrippa's Thermae (of which the plan is partly preserved and a broken dome still visible) show a more nearly symmetrical layout than the Campanian baths. Their main rooms are disposed roughly equally about the axis of a central block containing at least one large domed chamber. There are also a pair of large outward-facing semicircular niches with free-standing columns which suggest formalised outdoor space analogous to the courtyards of later imperial baths. If this is so, the essential elements of the great Thermae of the empire are present in embryo. Other notable Augustan structures on the Campus Martius were Agrippa's Pantheon, the Saepta Julia (a new and lavishly decorated voting enclosure) and two porticoes, the Porticus Octaviae and Porticus Philippi. Both the latter framed older temples and created spacious and dignified settings for them which were at the same time pleasant sheltered areas for Romans to meet and walk and enjoy the contrast with the narrow crowded streets and high buildings of the urban centre. The complex also contained many notable works of art and a pair of libraries, Greek and Latin. On the Esquiline, in the heart of the populated districts, the emperor's wife Livia built a new Macellum on an appropriately large scale (80 x 25m), consisting of the expected shops, with a portico, running round a courtyard with a large water basin in the middle. This, like so many other Augustan enterprises, was designed to bring up to date or supplement the facilities inherited from the Republic which were no longer adequate and were overdue for improvement—in this case the early second-century Macellum which lay behind the Basilica Paulli: of this we only know that it was grand enough to have a central *tholos*, which if later *macella* are any guide housed the water supply essential to this kind of market.

But in spite of all this, it was in the civic heart of Rome that the activity of Augustus was most striking. In the Republican forum, as has been said, he completed the Curia Julia and Basilica Julia (rebuilding the latter in A.D.12 after a fire). The Basilica Paulli received its last and most splendid reconstruction in 14 B.C.: the Aemilii were now very closely related to Augustus. At the north-west end, Augustus' stepson Tiberius in A.D.10 replaced Opimius' Temple of Concord with an unusual and ornate one of his own. The south-east end, hitherto not well defined, was closed off by the Temple of the Divine Julius. In front of this was a speaker's platform (*rostra*) which balanced the Republican *rostra* facing it down the length of the central paved space, and which also was adorned with the rams of captured ships—in this case those taken from Antony and Cleopatra at Actium. On either side of it stood Augustus' Actian and Parthian Arches. The latter was given added solemnity by having inscribed inside it the list of all the consuls since the foundation of the Republic, and was connected to the end of the Basilica Paulli by a kind of loggia named in memory of Augustus' adoptive sons Gaius and Lucius. As the visitor looked round, almost the only buildings of consequence not connected in a fairly direct way with the emperor were three temples, those of Vesta, Castor and Pollux, and Saturn; and of these Castor and Pollux had been substantially reconstructed by Tiberius, while Plancus who had built the new Temple of Saturn had eventually become one of the new regime's more distinguished supporters. The Julian presence was all-pervading, obliterating and replacing the past.

Probably Augustus' greatest architectural achievement was his own forum (fig. 17) lying at right angles to the Forum Iulium and immediately accessible from it. The basic idea is identical to that of Caesar: a temple on a high podium set on the long axis of a rectangle and dominating it from one end. But there is a subtle variation. Although the colonnades which line three sides of the forum are straight, there hide behind them two semicircular recesses. These are positioned so that the axis which joins them is aligned with the line of columns which constitute the front of the temple, and thus a cross-axis is introduced which would only be perceived from the steps of the temple or from within the apses themselves. It is interesting that deliberate use was made of curvilinear forms which are essentially at odds with the rectangular geometry of contemporary civic planning. Experience with the plasticity of concrete construction, or familiarity with the semicircle of the theatre, may be the influences here. The plan is slightly irregular at the eastern end, because Augustus had not been able to buy all the land he wanted. To conceal this, and to make the most of the available space, the temple was pushed right back against the massive eastern wall (cf. fig. 28). There is no sign of shops. Instead the forum was made into a kind of monument to the intertwined fortunes of Roma and the Julian family. The apses and colonnades contained two series of statues, with accompanying inscriptions, portraying the great figures of Roman history. One series, which began with Aeneas, son of Venus, depicted the ancestors and connections of the house of Caesar, the other, beginning with Romulus, son of Mars, all the rest. The message conveyed to the Roman people was even clearer than in the Republican forum, particularly as the temple itself had been vowed on the field of Philippi to Mars Ultor, Mars the Avenger— of Julius Caesar.

The elevated tone of the Forum Augustum was matched by its elevated style. The workmanship and detailing of the marble was exquisite, the taste impeccably classic. Over the porticoes was an attic storey, adorned with Caryatids which are close copies of those which support the celebrated south porch of the Erechtheum in Athens. A harking back to the glories of fifth and fourth century Greece is characteristic of other arts too in the Augustan period (although it is by no means limited to that period). The restrained but perfect work of that epoch was credited with a kind of moral excellence.[28] Its style was a model of clarity and apparent simplicity and stood in obvious contrast to the aggressiveness, emotionalism, self-display and self-indulgence which were displayed alike by art and politics in more recent times. From these it was Augustus' duty to protect his people. In connection with the building of Augustus' Palatine Temple of Apollo, it has been remarked 'As in rhetoric and literature, so also in the visual arts there was a belief in the moral effect produced by the classic form. The political will that was directed towards order, "purification", and "renewal" had here found adequate formal expression.'[29] If we look at Augustan public building as a whole, we see a style that is classicising, a building technique that is accomplished, though conservative, and an achievement that is based on tradition but is also revolutionary. It is revolutionary in the scale and quality of the facilities provided for the common people of Rome, and it set a standard for the whole empire. Augustan architecture is hardly original (except perhaps in its lavish use of marble), but as in statecraft, so in architecture Augustus drew on elements of the past to create something which transcended the sum of the parts and laid the basis for the following centuries.

IV. Imperial Rome

What we see in the Empire is essentially the flowering of the seeds sown in the Republican and Augustan periods. All the necessary ingredients were now present: the ability to construct large vaults and domes, the wealth to commission great buildings, and the social and political conditions which made it attractive to build them. For approximately fifty years following the death of Augustus little of consequence seems to happen. We can only guess whether this was due to the personalities and interests of the successors of Augustus, or whether it was the sheer scale of Augustus' activities, coupled with the strongly conservative tendencies apparent in the public architecture of his reign, which imposed this temporary standstill. With Nero, however, there begins a great surge of creativity running on to the time of Hadrian, followed by notable buildings from the third and fourth centuries. For the purposes of this chapter it will be possible to do no more than highlight the most important developments, particularly those shown in bath, basilica, and forum buildings.

The next Thermae after Agrippa's were those built by Nero in A.D.62 or 64 on the Campus Martius. They were rebuilt by Severus Alexander, but if the plan, known from Renaissance drawings, is Nero's, they introduced that exact symmetry which was lacking in Agrippa's. They possessed a central hall, about whose axis the two sets of rooms were balanced. This is a layout found in all the later imperial baths. As to construction, it is highly likely that the same concrete vaults and structural walling were used as are visible in the remains of the emperor's Domus Transitoria on the Palatine and Domus Aurea on the Esquiline; and one may take it for granted that the emperor whose name became a byword for luxury did not fail to make the architectural adornment rich and impressive.[30] These Thermae also seem to have included a gymnasium, an institution which had a cultural as well as an athletic connotation in the Greek world. This feature too reappears in subsequent Thermae, with their spacious courtyards and libraries. It is entirely natural that it should have been the Hellenophile Nero who gave the 'exercise yard' of the Pompeian baths a different dimension.

As it happened, the next two sets of imperial baths (fig. 19) either closely adjoined or actually overlay Nero's astonishing Domus Aurea.[31] Titus' Thermae, which were destroyed by a fire in 104, are relatively small, but conform to the precedent of Nero's with a symmetrical disposition of two suites of rooms either side of a central hall. This lay on the same axis as the monumental flight of steps which descended from the opposite side of the platform on which the whole complex is erected. Trajan built his Thermae a little further to the east and on a rather different orientation, which is repeated in all their successors and may be explained by the desirability of getting as much sun as possible into the *caldarium* in the afternoon and evening when the great majority of people bathed. These Thermae are the first really large set, measuring c. 330 x 315 m, an area four times the size of Titus'. They were the work of the architect Apollodorus of Damascus, whom we shall meet again in connection with Trajan's Forum, and show the same boldness of scale and conception as can be seen there. Substantial

BATHS OF TRAJAN

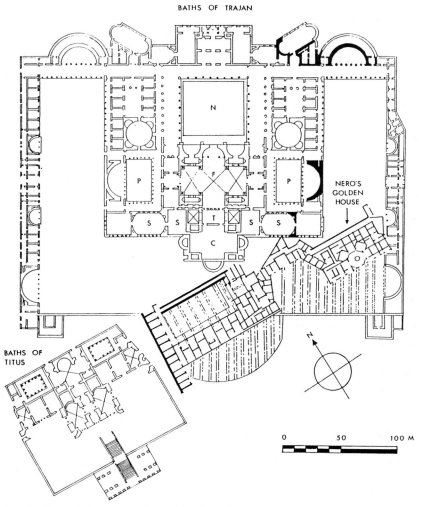

Fig. 19: Rome, Thermæ of Titus and Trajan: plan.

terracing was required for the huge platform on the slope of the hill behind the Domus Aurea, and it is this that has been responsible for preserving what we have of the latter.

Apollodorus created a structure so impressive and so well planned that it was, essentially, repeated by its two great successors, the Thermae of

Caracalla (212-217) and of Diocletian (298-306). The chief difference is that
in Trajan's the main block is attached to the north side of the rectangle of
the site, whereas in the other two it is free-standing and the space containing
gardens, walks, *exedrae*, *nymphaea* and even (in the case of Caracalla's)
libraries, completely encircled it. Entrance in each case was on the north-
east side, where in the centre there was a large open-air swimming-pool
(*natatio*). On either side of the central axis, of which the pool constituted
the first element, the layout was identical. First, flanking the pool came
a suite of rooms (in the case of Trajan's a rotunda amongst them) where
the dressing-rooms (*apodyteria*) must have been located. These gave on
to a palaestra, beyond which lay a sequence of variously shaped rooms
containing small plunge baths or basins, amongst them probably a Turkish
bath (*laconicum*). Finally the bather reached the *caldarium* lying at the
southern end of the central axis. This constituted the heart of the range
of hot rooms and was the largest and most elaborate of them, either apsed
and niched or (in the case of Caracalla's) actually circular. Progress could
then be made back along the axis towards the *natatio*, by way first of the
tepidarium, which formed a sort of intervening vestibule, and then across
the vast rectangular *frigidarium* at the heart of the whole complex.

     In all three examples this huge hall was cross-vaulted in three bays and
supported on massive piers. Some idea of the character of such a space can
be had from the church of S.Maria degli Angeli, remodelled by Michelangelo from the central hall of the Thermae of Diocletian. The presence of
columns and all the trappings of traditional architectural vocabulary was
structurally unnecessary. Walls likewise could be done away with, and
were. Space became fluid, as subsidiary shapes and bays were fashioned
around and between the supporting skeleton of the great vaulted roofs.
The impressiveness of the complicated perspectives that were offered by
the magnificent interiors of the central rooms, as they flowed one into the
other, gleaming with mosaic, exotic marble and statuary, must have been
overwhelming. The exteriors, too, were not neglected, but had applied
to them the multi-tiered ranks of columns and niches which were found
in *nymphaea* and other ornamental façades, and originate in the elaborate
compositions of the *scaenae frontes* of Roman theatres (see pp. 103f). Thus
the great Roman bath-buildings represent a fusion of the native utilitarian
tradition, which developed the concrete on which their lofty vaults and
baroque curves depended, with the quite different tradition of late Hellenistic playfulness with the orders, itself baroque in a different way.[32] And
perhaps most important of all, they affirmed the primacy of interior over
exterior.

     These *frigidaria* were in effect large basilicas—wide, rectangular public halls. They could have possessed galleries, though it seems that they did not. It is interesting, therefore, that the very same Apollodorus who built a pier-supported, concrete-vaulted hall for Trajan's Thermae preferred a much more conservative solution for the enormous Basilica Ulpia which lay across one end of the new forum built by Trajan between 106 and 113 to the north of the Forum Augustum (fig. 17 and pl. 10). This was innovative in possessing an apse at each end, and in its size (c. 60 x 120m, or 170m into the apses), but was otherwise no different from the basilicas of the Republic. It was timber-roofed and had a double aisle and gallery running round all four sides, whose columns were of coloured marble surmounted by a frieze of Victories depicted in the act of adorning candelabra or sacrificing. A taller order of grey granite columns ran round each apse. Outside, as a coin of Trajan reveals, its three doors to the forum were given elaborate architectural treatment. In addition, the central porch carried a triumphal quadriga, left and right was other statuary on the theme of victory, and a figured relief frieze[33] ran the whole length of the attic storey. The impact of this building was such that its plan was copied in basilicas at places as far apart as Timgad and Silchester.

Behind and adjoining the basilica were two libraries (which did make some use of concrete construction) and between them the Column of Trajan with its famous continuous spiral frieze depicting the details of the Dacian War, of which the basilica and forum were the triumphal monument. It also, and perhaps (if one may judge from its inscription)[34] primarily, served to remind Rome just how huge a building enterprise this was. To make way for the whole complex Trajan cut deeply into the slopes of the Quirinal, a process begun already by Augustus, and entirely removed a ridge that ran across to the Capitoline. The column marks the original height of this ridge. Trajan in fact was carrying out the idea that Caesar had once had of extending the monumental centre of the city north-westwards towards the Campus Martius; but although one has to admit that the conception was not new, the execution of it speaks of an assured mastery, on the largest scale, of both planning and construction. This mastery is one that we do not see before the Trajanic age in public buildings, but there can be no doubt that it had been learnt over the preceding fifty years, stimulated by the private architectural enterprises of Nero and Domitian.

The fact that the Basilica Ulpia formed the fourth side of Trajan's Forum placed it in the tradition of the Italic fora of the Republic, like that of Alba Fucens, and broke away from the newer configuration with a projecting temple at one end, which had been introduced by Caesar and adopted in the fora of Augustus and Nerva. Otherwise the relationship to the Forum of Augustus is close. The attics of the flanking porticoes repeat the caryatid motif, substituting figures of Dacian prisoners for the graceful maidens of the Erechtheum; the details of the architectural mouldings are very similar to Augustan work; and the semi-circular apses in the centre of each side echo those of the Forum Augustum (and are also identical in dimensions to those of the Basilica Ulpia, though this would not have been apparent on the spot). The entrance at the south end was by way of a triumphal arch, by now a familiar feature of fora. The segmental curve given to the south side seems to be due to a wish to accommodate the north apse of the Forum of Augustus without losing more than the minimum of space; but the adoption of this plan bears witness to the influence exerted by the fluid shapes which had been encouraged by the new building techniques and demonstrated in the Thermae of the period and in the palaces of Nero and Domitian.

Another traditional Italic feature of the Forum of Trajan is its association with shops. Behind the eastern apse, and divided from it by the street which ran behind the portico, was a hemicycle of shops in two storeys, built into the terracing which held back the hillside (fig. 20). Those at ground level opened directly on to the street, those above on to a corridor. This was lit by a row of windows which were framed by pilasters of stuccoed brick. Over them ran an entablature of the same material which was varied by a complicated sequence of segmental, triangular and broken pediments, reflecting the final demotion of the orders and their associated forms to a system of applied decoration. The larger openings of the ground floor were arched for strength, but the structural logic was concealed by applying jambs and architraves of travertine to the rectangular lower part of the opening and walling in the top segment, leaving only a small squarish window. Built into the slope of the hill above these is a complex of irregular streets and stairways on three different levels, containing over a hundred more shops and a vaulted market hall. The construction is in what is now established as the standard brick-faced concrete of the imperial period, in contrast to the old-fashioned (and doubtless expensive) cut stone and timber of the Basilica and Forum. The market-hall itself (pl. 11) is a descendant of a type of building known from Republican Italy, a covered, utilitarian space with side rooms. Ferentinum offers a very clear example, to be dated c.100 B.C., with a plain barrel-vault. Trajan's market hall shows how far the techniques of concrete roofing had come. The groined cross-vaulting gives height and admits light to the hall, while the wall below needs to be no more than a series of piers joined by arches, in which the shops are set in the way described above. The state of preservation, not only of the hall, but of the whole of the area, is a remarkable tribute to the quality of design and construction which the Romans were now routinely

Fig. 20: Rome, Trajan's Market: isometric drawing.

capable of producing. Nowhere else can one get a more vivid feel of what ancient Rome was really like as an urban environment.

Trajan's was the last of the series of imperial fora. No more great improvements were made to the centre of the capital until in 307 Maxentius started the construction of a new basilica (Basilica Nova) alongside the Sacred Way between the republican forum and the Arch of Titus. He died before it was finished, and the building was dedicated by the senate to Constantine, who altered the main axis from 'long' to 'short' by adding a porch in the middle of the side towards the Sacred Way, and an apse opposite it. Even in its ruined state the basilica cannot fail to impress the modern visitor with its demonstration of the capabilities of Roman concrete. The architects abandoned the traditional basilica form, and adopted that of the *frigidaria* of the great imperial baths. The cross-vaulted roof sprang from eight piers fronted by single huge columns of Proconnesian marble, and these piers were in their turn supported by three vast barrel-vaulted bays, of a lesser height than the main hall, at each side. The principle is exactly that of a Gothic cathedral. What we see today are the three bays of the north-east side, colossal enough in themselves; but the original size of the building was 100 x 65m of which the central nave, 35m high, was 80 x 25m. The nave was thus almost exactly the same width as the naves of the main halls of the baths of Caracalla and Diocletian, but almost a third longer. At the same time the increased depth of the lateral bays of Constantine's basilica, coupled with the height of their vaults, meant that the feeling of space and width was far greater. The building must have seemed much loftier, squarer and less cluttered than the Ulpia with its double-storeyed colonnaded side aisles and masked apses. Maxentius intended the north-west apse of his basilica to contain a colossal statue of himself. It must be virtually certain that when Constantine altered the axis of the building, he placed his own colossal statue in the new north-east apse (and fragments of such a statue are known). The tendency for the emperor to dominate the civic, as well as the constitutional and military, aspects of the state has here received open expression. The adoption of the basilica as a hall for worship of the Christian god was brought about not merely by practical considerations, but by the symbolic association of the great hall with reverence for the ruler.

V. *Rome and the Provinces*

Roman architecture is not simply the architecture of Rome and Italy, but a style that became diffused both east and west as a result of the establishment of the Roman empire. The buildings of the capital provided models for other places, particularly in the western and African provinces where the creation of towns was the most spectacular effect of the spread of Roman power. The dominant classes of these areas adopted Roman patterns of social behaviour and political organisation, and with them the need for physical structures to express urban identity and make possible a version of the Graeco-Italic lifestyle. So we find in distant Britain a splendid, if not entirely typical, bath-building at Aquae Sulis (Bath) and a huge basilica, 130m long, at Londinium (London). The mutation of the civic basilica into church or imperial audience-hall [35] can be vividly glimpsed at Augusta Treverorum (Trier) where there survives in a remarkable state of preservation the basilica which formed part of the imperial palace of Constantinian times (pl. 12). Strictly speaking it is not a public building, but it is descended from the type of basilica whose axis ran from its entrance to an apse or tribunal opposite (Pompeii, Fanum Fortunae, Maxentius' in Rome). Its purpose was to enthrone the emperor in state in the apse, and it is for this reason that the windows in that part of the building were made less tall than those in the nave, so that the false perspective would exaggerate the size of the emperor. This use of perspective, and the ordered rhythm of the plain arcades, suggest an architecture that is already starting to develop further and break away from the methods and objectives of the previous two hundred years.

In the African provinces, Lepcis Magna (pp. 23ff) serves as a good example of the way a provincial town could feel the currents from Italy. Lepcis was an old Punic trading station, but the first surviving remains are those of the very late Republic and Augustan periods. Over a span of some fifty to seventy years the leading citizens of the town, with distinctly non-Roman names like Iddibal and Bommelqart, behaved exactly like their metropolitan counterparts in endowing their native city with a forum and associated buildings of good Italic type. As completed at the end of this period, the Old Forum of Lepcis had three temples side by side at its head, all with high podia of Italic style (fig. 21). Opposite these temples was built a single-aisled basilica, which although its long axis lay parallel to this side of the forum was entered, like the basilica of Pompeii, from one end. The complex of temple-forum-basilica is the basic ingredient of numerous Italic town centres, and its occurrence here, in regular form, is a striking indication of the process of Romanisation. The *curia* of Lepcis also dates from this same period. It is placed at one corner of the forum, facing the entrance to the basilica, and strongly resembles a temple: raised on a podium and having a columned porch, it was set within a compact porticoed court in almost exactly the same way, in miniature, as the Temple of Mars Ultor. This arrangement recalls the fact that the Roman senate customarily met in a temple (cf. p. 79).

Lepcis also has a particularly fine specimen of the *macellum* or food-market, built in 8 B.C. (fig. 22) of the same limestone that is used for all

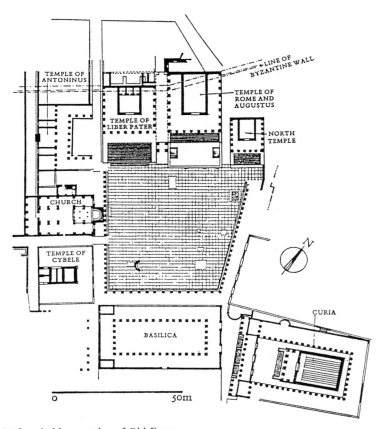

Fig. 21: Lepcis Magna: plan of Old Forum.

these early buildings. The central *tholos* (here duplicated) was a feature of
the Macellum at Rome and occurs elsewhere later, as for example at Pompeii and Puteoli. The Lepcis *tholoi* are octagonal, their exterior columns a
stumpy Ionic, bearing a heavy plain entablature of no canonical form, while
the interior drum is arcaded and has a simple relief cornice supported by
shallow pilasters of vaguely Corinthian type to articulate it. We are clearly
in the presence of 'provincial' art, away from but imitating the mainstream.
But by the time of Hadrian (A.D.117–138) the increasing prosperity of the
town and the wider availability of fine marble (and craftsmen to work it)
from elsewhere, changed all that. The turning-point is marked by the Hadri-

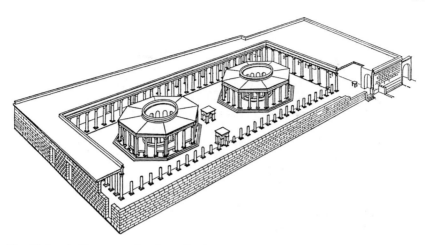

Fig. 22: Lepcis Magna, market (*macellum*): restored view.

anic Baths, planned after the model of the imperial bath-buildings of Rome. They were large and symmetrical, and made extensive use of imported materials, although the concrete vaulting so confidently handled in Rome by this time is not much in evidence.

The third stage in this brief case-history is the reign of Septimius Severus (193–211), who was a native of Lepcis and lavished money on his home town (cf. p. 25 and pl. 2). Amongst the results was a complete new forum, whose layout will cause no surprise, even though Rome itself had no forum on exactly this pattern. At one end there was a temple to the Severan dynasty which thrust forward its lofty podium and unusual spreading steps along the axis of the space; at the other lay a basilica with a wedge-shaped row of shops cunningly placed between it and the portico that surrounded the forum in order to mask the fact that (because of the irregular site) the basilica was not quite parallel to the portico. The main entrance to the basilica was through a semi-circular exedra which opened off this portico directly opposite the temple. It thus established a strong axiality but at the same time concealed by its lack of rectangularity the obliqueness of the basilica. Just as in the Forum of Trajan, the semicircular form was picked up inside the basilica, which was on the pattern of the Ulpia, double-apsed, timber-roofed, and galleried—except that the gallery did not run across the building, so that the double tier of columns bracketed to the wall around the curve of each apse was fully visible. The central span, at 19m, was only 3m less than that of the Ulpia, and the construction was similarly conservative, in cut stone masonry with only the apses and the exedra at the entrance made of rubble concrete faced with small squared blocks.

The detailing of the marble used for bases, columns, capitals and entablature shows the influence of the Greek East, and Asia in particular. In the porticoes of the forum columns of green marble from Karystos were married with bases and capitals of white Pentelic marble. The capitals are a cross between the 'lotus' capitals of Pergamon and standard Corinthian, and the most striking and famous feature of these porticoes, namely that they are arcaded with the arches springing directly from the capitals of the columns, had been anticipated at Cyzicus in Hadrian's temple.[36] It seems that what we find at Lepcis, which may stand as a paradigm for much of the empire, is a fusion of large-scale forms developed in, and for, Italy, with a vocabulary of ornament that owes its inspiration, and tradition, to the Greek East. Such generalisations, of course, must be applied with caution, as the 'Hunting Baths' at Lepcis, of roughly the same date, warn us. These are a corrective to the idea that all bath-buildings, at least after the first century, are vast people's palaces of centralised design that conceal their structure behind the trappings of traditional architectural ornament. The 'Hunting Baths', like the majority of modest establishments in the Roman empire, resembled more the *balnea* of Pompeii than the Thermae of Trajan. The stark concrete domes and vaults are simply the result of functional planning and functional construction. This remarkable exterior is the proof of the turning inside out of traditional architecture.

If we turn to the East itself, and to a city that could reasonably be considered the most important of Asia Minor under the Empire, we find that the Greeks were ready to take back ideas which they had originally given to the Romans and the Romans had developed. Ephesus, like very many Greek cities, had a depth of culture and a length of architectural history that made the Romans seem parvenus. As Vitruvius makes clear,[37] most of the architectural inheritance of late Republican Italy came from Greece, and the Greeks were therefore in quite a different relationship to Rome from other, more newly civilised, areas of the empire. The planning ideas that informed the imperial fora at Rome had their roots in the Hellenistic world. When the 'Staatsmarkt' or civic agora of Ephesus was rebuilt in Augustan times, it did not become like an Italic forum: the temple (possibly of Artemis)[38] was erected in the middle and not at one end; the basilica which ran all the way down one side was so long and narrow as to be more like an enclosed stoa; and the Bouleuterion (= *curia*) and the shrines of Roma, Divus Julius, and Augustus were neatly and asymmetrically tucked away behind the basilica without any obvious relationship to the main space of the agora.

On the other hand, the Roman development of the thermal bath was enthusiastically accepted. Between the late first century A.D. and the middle of the second, Ephesus acquired no less than three sets of bath-buildings of 'imperial' type, all with large palaestrae built in (Harbour Baths, East Baths and Baths of Vedius). Vaulted in mortared rubble-work or brick, their plans represent local variations on the standard Roman scheme. Most important, however, is their incorporation of the Greek *gymnasium*, a feature discussed above [39] in connection with Nero's Thermae in Rome. To this are due not only the substantial palaestrae, and in the case of the Harbour Baths an attached covered running-track[40], but also the open-sided halls or large rectangular niches which the Germans have christened 'Marmorsaale'. A screen of columns ran across the long open side, and the other three walls were covered with elaborate architectural compositions in two orders of columns with *aediculae*, niches, statuary, and so on. The intention was presumably to provide a quiet spot where one could turn over one's thoughts in a suitably uplifting setting, or admire the sculpture as in a museum.

One can get some idea of the flavour of this kind of façade architecture from the Library of Celsus (c.A.D.135), which can truly be termed baroque in its restless in-and-out movement and particularly in the instability created by the arrangement of the *aediculae* (pl. 13). The architect has quite deliberately disrupted the normal placing one above the other and has also made play with the alternation of round and triangular pediments. The latter feature goes back to Hellenistic times and it is hard to maintain that this kind of architecture owes much to Rome apart from the political and economic conditions which permitted it to be built. Inside (to conclude with a type of public building not so far discussed here) the library was less adventurous and resembled others that are known, e.g. at Timgad (p. 22). It was rectangular, with an apse for statuary opposite the door, and had three tiers of rectangular niches in the walls to hold bookcases. Access to these was by two galleries supported by a double tier of columns which ran in front of the lower two rows of niches. The Library of Celsus was in fact his funerary monument, as he was buried in a vaulted chamber below the apse; and since tombs are definitely not public buildings, this seems as appropriate a place as any to end this glance at Roman architecture in the provinces of the empire.

NOTES

1. Livy 41.27 (174 B.C.)

2. Horace, *Epistles* 2.1.156.

3. A theatre was later built on the site of the Republican basilica (see pl. 5).

4. For a full account, see F.E.Brown, *Cosa: the Making of a Roman Town* (Ann Arbor 1980).

5. Herdonia has a *macellum* of very similar plan, Saepinum a hexagonal one.

6. ILLRP 528 = ILS 5348.

7. That is, capable of withstanding pressure, as in a siphon. (See further ch. 5).

8. This material, found in the regions immediately north and south of Naples, is nowadays called pozzolana (from the modern name of Puteoli). See Vitruvius 2.6.1.

9. G.Gullini in *Architecture et Société de l'Archaisme grecque à la Fin de la République romaine* (Rome 1983), 119–189.

10. Livy 36.36.3-4.

11. The dating to 174 accepted by L.Crema, *L'Architettura romana* (Torino 1959) 61, G.Gullini (n.9 above), and others; for doubts, L.Richardson AJA 80 (1976), 57 ff.

12. Vitruvius 2.8.1.

13. F.Coarelli, PBSR 45 (1977), 1-19.

14. Vitruvius 2.8.8-9.

15. AE 1971.61. See JRS 66 (1976), 17f. The man's name was L. Cornelius.

16. Asconius 33C.

17. Vitruvius 5.2.

18. The Porcia was burnt in 52 B.C. along with the Curia Hostilia and never rebuilt; the Sempronia was replaced by the Julia. On the identification of the Basilica Aemilia, see below, note 24.

19. Suetonius, *Divus Augustus* 29.1.

20. *Captivi* 815. The same reference indicates the existence close by of the *macellum*, by mentioning the stink of bad fish.

21. See Livy 26.27.2, 27.11.16.

22. See F. Coarelli, *Il Foro Romano, II: Periodo Repubblicano e Augusteo* (Rome 1985), 146-152.

23. Vitruvius 5.1.6-10.

24. Pliny, *Natural History* 36.49; 102. Recent excavations in the Forum Romanum have shown that the Basilica Aemilia was not, as used to be thought, and as marked on our figures 16 and 17, the same building as the Basilica Paulli (which is always so called in the literary sources): see M. Steinby, *Arctos* 21 (1987), 172ff.

25. See the colourful description of Strabo 5.3.8.

26. Seneca, *Moral Epistles* 86.

27. Pliny, *Natural History* 9.54; 26.3.

28. See the vivid expression of this view in relation to oratory by Dionysius of Halicarnassus (a contemporary of Augustus), *On the Ancient Orators* 1-3.

29. P.Zanker 'Der Apollontempel auf dem Palatin' in K.de Fine Licht (ed.), *Città e Architettura nella Roma imperiale* (Odense 1983), 21-40.

30. Martial 7.34.

31. See A.Boëthius, *The Golden House of Nero* (Ann Arbor 1960).

32. M.Lyttelton, *Baroque Architecture in Classical Antiquity* (London 1974), chh. 1 and 2.

33. This frieze is almost certainly to be identified with that known as the Great Trajanic Frieze, large portions of which have been preserved in the Arch of Constantine. Size, scale and subject-matter are all highly appropriate.

34. ILS 294.

35. Cf. J.B.Ward-Perkins, 'Constantine and the origins of the Christian basilica', PBSR 22 (1954), 69-90.

36. The motif, which breaks the fundamental 'grammar' of the orders, is found in painted form at Pompeii 150 years earlier still, in the Villa of the Mysteries.

37. See pp. 3f above.

38. F.Felten 'Heiligtümer oder Märkte?' *Antike Kunst* 26 (1983), 95 ff.

39. P. 52 above.

40. See Vitruvius 5.11.3-4.

3. Religious Buildings

Ian M. Barton

If you look up the word *templum* in a Latin dictionary, you will find its essential meanings given something like this:

> (1) The area of sky or land defined ... by the augur, within which he took the auspices. (2) A piece of ground demarcated and consecrated by the augurs for the taking of auspices; ... a sacred precinct.[1]

From the idea of an enclosure dedicated to religious purposes, the meaning is extended to denote the building which was usually (in classical times) the dominant feature of the site. For this the correct term is *aedes*, and this is the term invariably used by Vitruvius in his prescriptions for the building of temples in Books 3 and 4. Many of the buildings in Rome which we call 'temples' are regularly referred to in inscriptions and by Latin authors as *aedes*, and the distinction is clear in an inscription of the middle of the second century A.D. which refers to a meeting as being held 'in templo divorum in aede divi Titi'[2]—'in the sacred precinct of the deified emperors, in the shrine of deified Titus'. In other words, it is possible to have a *templum* without an *aedes*, but an *aedes* can only stand within a *templum*.

There is nothing particularly exceptional about the Roman practice of enclosing an *aedes* within a *templum*: in Greek sanctuaries, it was the sacred area (*temenos*) which came first and the temple (*naos*) was a later adornment, and we may compare the Christian practice of building churches in a churchyard. The essential feature for the conduct of religious ritual, both in Greek and Roman religion, was an altar (*ara*) at which sacrifices were offered to the divinity. This always stood in the open, and in Roman temples was regularly placed directly in front of the steps which led up to the façade of the *aedes*. It is important to realise that classical temple buildings were not intended to house congregations of worshippers; their essential purpose was to accommodate the statue of the god in a room called the *cella*, and secondarily to act as a storehouse for the offerings made to the shrine.

Most Greek sanctuaries developed in a fairly haphazard manner over many centuries and therefore show little evidence of conscious planning; often there is not even any clear relation between the altar and the temple building. But in Hellenistic times, from about the end of the fourth century B.C., attempts began to be made to plan a temple and its surrounding enclosure as an artistic whole, with some regard to the principles of symmetry and axiality—that is, siting the temple building on the centre line of a regularly planned enclosure. This practice was taken up and developed by Roman architects, who in the last two centuries of the Roman Republic sought to combine the Hellenistic Greek tradition of temple architecture, with which the growth of the Roman empire brought them into contact, with the older Italic tradition which at Rome goes back to the sixth century B.C., the period of the Etruscan kings.

By universal consent, the oldest religious building of the Roman Republic was the triple temple of Jupiter, Juno and Minerva on the Capitoline hill—the *Capitolium*, traditionally founded by the Etruscan kings and dedicated by the consuls in the first year of the new Republic (509 B.C.).[3] Although this venerable building was several times burnt and reconstructed, it seems always to have retained its original plan, which can be restored with some certainty and conforms well with Vitruvius' description of his 'Tuscan' temple.[4] Since similar arrangements are found in many temples in Italian towns between the sixth and second centuries B.C., it is clear that we have here a well-established indigenous type of temple plan, quite different in its design and effect from the peripteral temples of classical and Hellenistic Greece, with their surrounding colonnades on a low platform with steps all round. Its distinctive features (fig. 23) are the high podium approached only by a broad flight of steps in front; the deep and broad entrance porch (according to Vitruvius)[5] the ratio of breadth to length should be 5:6, and the porch should occupy half the total length); the tripartite division of the rear part of the building—either a triple cella or a single

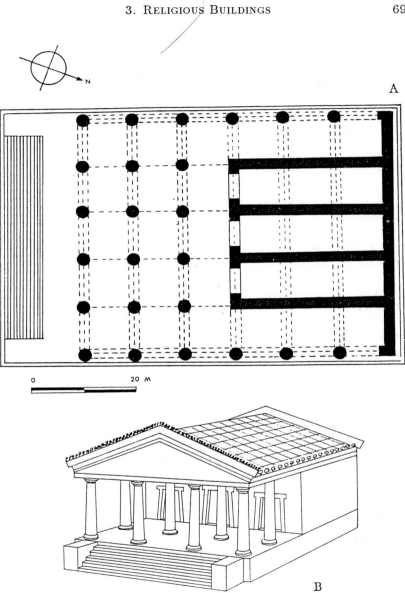

Fig. 23: (a) Rome: plan of Capitoline Temple; (b) restored view of a typical Etruscan
    temple.

cella flanked by 'wings' (*alae*); and the solid back wall running the whole width of the podium. It can be clearly seen from the diagrams that this type of plan throws the emphasis on to the façade of the temple, which will inevitably dominate the space in front of it. This is in marked contrast with the effect of a peripteral Greek temple, which is designed to be walked round and viewed from all directions, with no particular emphasis on the front.

The temples at Cosa (cf. p. 13) provide a good example of the traditional plan. Although they seem to have been built about a century after the original foundation of the colony, towards the middle of the second century B.C., they are completely Italic in design. The Capitolium, on the south-western hilltop, has the expected triple cella, with the side walls projecting to form *antae* between which is a pair of columns; four columns stand in front—the arrangement called prostyle (fig. 24). In the smaller temples can be seen various simplifications of the plan: what they have in common is their frontality. The widely spaced columns of this type of temple can only have supported a timber entablature with revetments of terracotta, and this is what Vitruvius describes in 4.7, where he speaks of 'beams fastened together' (*trabes compactiles*) and casings (*antepagmenta*) on the ends of projecting beams (*traiecturae mutulorum*).[6] Remains of such features from Cosa and elsewhere show considerable decorative elaboration and indicate that the overall effect must have been extremely rich.

By the second century B.C., however, temples like those at Cosa were already old-fashioned. Livy tells us[7] that Greek embellishments were first introduced into Roman buildings by Marcellus, the conqueror of Syracuse (212 B.C.); and the eastern campaigns of Roman generals in the next half-century led to an influx of Greek artists and works of art. In 146 B.C., the year in which Greek independence ended with the sack of Corinth, the Temple of Jupiter Stator was founded by Metellus Macedonicus; he commissioned a Greek architect, Hermodorus of Salamis, and it was the first temple in Rome to be built entirely of marble.[8] Nothing survives of the structure, but its plan is known from the *Forma Urbis*, and shows an interesting compromise between Greek and Italic (fig. 25). Like a Greek temple, it has a long narrow cella with a prostyle porch and colonnades on the flanks, but the flanking colonnades are stopped by extensions of the rear wall of the cella, so that the temple fails to be fully peripteral (what Vitruvius[9] calls *ambulatio sine postico facta*—'a covered walk without a rear portion'). In appearance it no doubt resembled other late Republican temples which still survive, like the row of temples in Largo Argentina or the two well-preserved temples in the Forum Boarium (pl. 14), which are probably to be identified as the Temple of Hercules Victor (the round

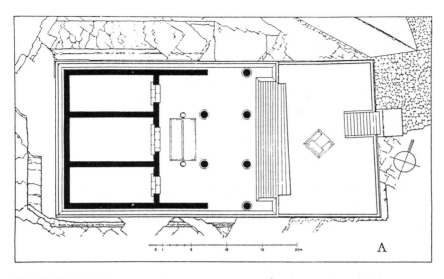

Fig. 24: Cosa, Capitolium: (a) restored plan; (b) restored perspective view.

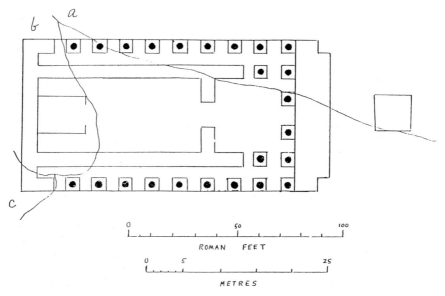

Fig. 25: Rome, Temple of Jupiter Stator: plan, restored after the Forma Urbis—a, b, c
mark the extant fragments.

temple) and the Temple of Portunus (formerly called 'Fortuna Virilis').[10]

These and other temples of the period show architects using and adapt-
ing the classical orders of Greek architecture—Doric, Ionic and the variety
of the latter which has the Corinthian capital. A good example of Roman
Doric is the Temple of Hercules at Cori in Latium, probably built c.100
B.C. (pl. 15). It stands on a podium, and its front half is occupied by a
porch with four columns on the front and two returning on each side. The
cella occupies the whole width of the podium. The Doric columns are much
slenderer than in classical Greek architecture, the height being about seven
times the diameter; they stand on low bases and their capitals are quite
insignificant. The entablature too is much lighter than in classical Doric,
and in the frieze there are three triglyphs to each intercolumniation. For
an example of Roman Ionic, we may look at the Temple of Portunus mentioned above. It too stands on a podium approached by steps at the front
and has a tetrastyle (i.e. four-column) porch, though in this case there is
a return of one column only. The bases and capitals are modelled on the
canonical classical designs, but again the capitals are relatively small. The
entablature is light and plain. The most striking feature of this temple is
the way in which the row of flanking columns is continued in the form of

half-columns engaged in the side walls of the cella and round the back. This arrangement ('pseudoperipteral') gives the effect of a peripteral building, four columns by seven, while allowing the cella to occupy the full width of the podium.

Of the temples so far mentioned, the round temple of Hercules Victor is the most Hellenistic in appearance. Round buildings (*tholoi*) occur occasionally in Greek architecture, and this one, with its ring of twenty Corinthian columns on a low stepped podium surrounding a circular cella of marble masonry, is clearly inspired by these: in fact, if the date currently assigned (c.120 B.C.) is correct, it might well have been designed by a Greek architect such as Hermodorus. There is certainly nothing Italic about it, unless it be the fact that it is a temple—for *tholoi* in Greek sanctuaries apparently were not. In Roman architecture the exemplar for round temples was the *aedes Vestae* in the Forum, containing the civic hearth (of which the goddess Vesta was a personification). The existing building is a reconstruction of the late second century A.D., but it was Roman tradition that it reproduced the shape of the earliest thatched huts on the site of Rome.[11] The pleasing effect of such round buildings no doubt contributed to their popularity, and they were not restricted to the cult of Vesta. Most conformed to Italic practice to the extent of being raised on a podium with steps only at the front: examples are to be found in Largo Argentina (Temple B, mid-second century B.C.) and at Tibur (Tivoli: the so-called 'Temple of Vesta', early first century B.C.). The latter is notable for the elegance of its Corinthian capitals, which were used in the late eighteenth century by Sir John Soane as the model for his building of the Bank of England.

Before leaving the temple architecture of the Republic, something should be said about a group of spectacular monuments laid out in Latium between the late second century and the middle of the first century B.C. Of these the grandest was the sanctuary of Fortuna Primigenia at Praeneste (Palestrina), where the hillside behind an older temple, which stood in what was probably the town's forum, was elaborately terraced on no fewer than seven levels, connected by ramps and staircases, with colonnades fronting long rows of vaulted rooms (fig. 26). The whole layout was strictly symmetrical, and culminated in a theatral area (cf. p. 101) with, at the top of its *cavea*, and exactly on the central axis, a round temple, over 60 metres above the level of the forum. Other elaborate complexes which involved the construction of terraces raised on huge vaults are the sanctuaries of Jupiter Anxur at Tarracina (Terracina) and of Hercules Victor at Tibur. The latter, which is dated c.50 B.C., also includes a theatre, and was perhaps deliberately designed by the Tiburtini to compete with their Praenestine neighbours. It has been usual to regard the sanctuary of

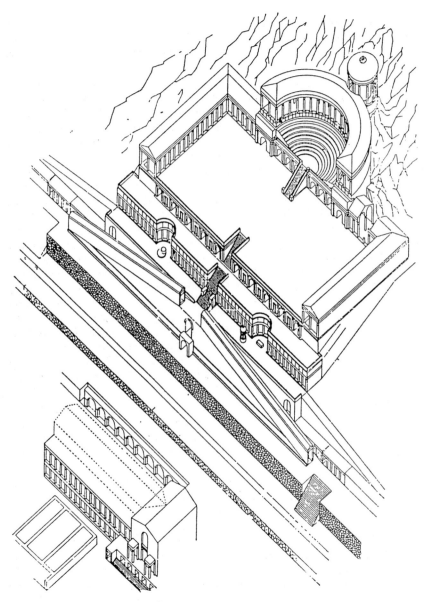

Fig. 26: Praeneste, Sanctuary of Fortuna Primigenia: restored axonometric plan.

Fortuna as a monument of the period after Praeneste was sacked during the civil war between Sulla and the followers of Marius and was then re-founded as a veteran colony (82/1 B.C.), but some recent scholars have suggested a date in the second half of the second century B.C.

However that may be, the existence of these enormous projects necessarily raises the question of who paid for them and why. There is a good deal of evidence to suggest that many of the major temples in Rome were built from the spoils of war (*de manubiis*) by successful generals like Marcellus and Metellus: the *elogium* (memorial inscription) of Marius recorded 'de manubiis Cimbris et Teuton(is) aedem Honori et Virtuti victor fecit'[12]— 'from the spoils taken from the Cimbri and Teutoni he built as victor a temple to Honour and Courage'. We know from Vitruvius[13] that this temple was *sine postico* and that the architect was a Roman named C. Mucius. Other events could also be commemorated in this way: the Temple of Concord is said to have been founded to mark the end of a period of civil strife; that of the Great Mother (Magna Mater) in obedience to an oracle found in the Sibylline Books at a crisis of the Second Punic War. In such cases the building was presumably paid for out of public funds on the authority of the Senate. But what of temples outside Rome? Unfortunately we have very little evidence for the Republican period, but it is reasonable to suppose that the appearance of large complexes in towns near Rome after the middle of the second century B.C. is due to the increasing prosperity of Italy that resulted from Rome's overseas expansion. Leading families of places like Praeneste and Tibur were now acquiring the kind of wealth which would make it possible for them to contribute lavishly to the adornment of their home towns, and the availability of this wealth would encourage the town councils to embark on major 'prestige' projects like those described above.

There was also a political dimension to these late Republican building programmes. Praeneste was one of a number of towns which had to receive a colony of veteran soldiers after Sulla's victory in the civil war of the 80s. At Pompeii the large temple at the head of the Forum (fig. 14) was remodelled at this time, probably to mark the town's transition to the status of a Roman citizen colony by converting it into a temple of the Capitoline cult of Jupiter, Juno and Minerva. This is unlikely to have been an isolated example. The institution of the Capitoline cult was a visible symbol of the changed status of the place. At Rome itself, building served the political ambitions of leading senators. In some cases the dedication of a temple might have a propaganda purpose: in 121 B.C. the consul L. Opimius marked his violent suppression of C. Gracchus and his party by restoring the Temple of Concord;[14] Pompey commemorated (probably) his illegal triumph of 80 B.C. by founding a temple of Hercules, as a kind of manifesto of his military ambitions;[15] and after securing Cicero's exile in 58 B.C. his enemy Clodius consecrated part of the site of his house as a temple of Liberty.[16]

The political potential of temple building was exploited, as never before or after his time, by Augustus. In the official account of his achievements, the *Res Gestae*, he claims to have restored eighty-two 'temples of the gods' (*templa deum*) in the year of his sixth consulship (28 B.C.) and lists another dozen which he built (though at least some of these were rebuildings of older temples).[17] This great programme for the beautification of the city advertised the return of peace and prosperity under the new régime in general, but there was special value in temple building as an indication of the favour of the gods.[18] Aesthetically too the temples of the Augustan age mark an important stage in the development of classical architecture, with the creation of Corinthian as a separate order in its own right, instead of a mere variation of Ionic as it had been in Hellenistic practice. Vitruvius, writing early in the reign of Augustus, could still say that Corinthian lacked a system of its own (*propriam institutionem*) for the entablature but could have either Doric or Ionic arrangements above the capitals.[19] The former strange-looking combination is actually found in a temple of Italic plan (fig. 27) at Paestum (a Roman colony since 273), where it probably dates from a reconstruction of c.100 B.C. But by the time Vitruvius' treatise was published this statement was already out of date: the surviving remains of the Temple of Apollo *in Circo*, which must have been finished by c.20 B.C., already show a distinctive type of entablature with carved decoration on the four-stepped architrave, a richly decorated frieze and—the most distinctive feature of Roman Corinthian—projecting S-shaped brackets (called modillions) to support the cornice. Although there is considerable variation in the details of the design, nearly all the principal temples of the Augustan age and the next two centuries, both in Rome and in the provinces of the Empire, were to be conceived in accordance with these principles.

The greatest of the Augustan temples in Rome is the Temple of Mars the Avenger (*Mars Ultor*) which dominated the new Forum of Augustus. The idea of a regular enclosed space surrounding a temple which is sometimes, but not always, placed on its central axis goes back, as was said above, to the Hellenistic period: well-known examples are the sanctuary of Athene Polias at Priene in Asia Minor and, in Italy, the Temple of Apollo at Pompeii. In these, however, the temple building was usually free-standing in accordance with the Greek preference for viewing a building from all round. The Forum Augustum, like its predecessor, the Forum Iulium begun by Julius Caesar, added the Italic characteristic of frontality to the tentative axiality of Hellenistic planners to produce a symmetrical enclosed

Fig. 27: Paestum, Republican temple: restored drawing of entablature.

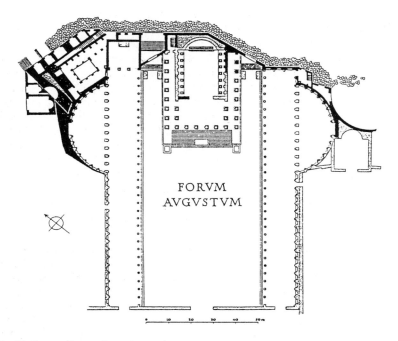

FORVM
AVGVSTVM

Fig. 28: Rome, Forum Augustum: plan.

space dominated from the end opposite the entrance by the imposing façade of the temple (fig. 28). The dedications chosen for these temples again emphasise the political aspect of religious architecture: in the Forum Julium, the Temple of Venus Genetrix advertised the legendary descent of the Julian house (*gens Iulia*) from the goddess; in the Forum Augustum, the Temple of Mars Ultor fulfilled a vow made at the time of the Battle of Philippi (42 B.C.) to commemorate the avenging of Caesar's murder by the defeat of Brutus and Cassius. It also became the repository of the standards recovered by Augustus from the Parthians in 20 B.C.—yet another political message.

The two temples had similar plans (peripteral *sine postico*), that of Mars being considerably larger. The original design of the superstructure of the Temple of Venus is unknown, since the existing remains belong to a reconstruction of Trajan's time (cf. p. 89 below). The Temple of Mars (eventually completed in 2 B.C.) shows the assured combination of Greek and Roman traditions which characterises the best of Augustan art (cf. the

Ara Pacis Augustae, built between 13 and 9 B.C., at about the time that work was starting on the new Forum). It stands on a high podium approached in front by a broad flight of steps (pl. 16). On the façade eight Corinthian columns, over 15m high, supported a three-stepped architrave and apparently a plain frieze (thus reverting to the older Ionic practice); but the cornice again had S-shaped modillions. The pediment is known from an ancient relief to have contained sculpture, representing Mars and other divinities. The colonnade was continued along the flanks until stopped by the rear wall, which is also the back wall of the precinct; here a Corinthian pilaster responds to each side colonnade. The sides, like the façade, have eight columns, so that the plan of the temple is nearly square (approximately 38 x 40m). There was also a return of two columns in the porch behind the façade columns next to the corners, so creating a spacious entrance porch. Inside the temple the cella was flanked by internal columns and terminated in a central apse which contained statues of Mars, Venus and Divus Iulius.

We happen to have a number of allusions to the Temple of Mars Ultor which well illustrate the variety of functions which a temple could fulfil. Quite apart from the religious ceremonies conducted at the altar, which would have stood on the central axis of the enclosure in front of the *aedes*, we are told that it was designated as the place where youths were enrolled for military training, the starting-point for governors departing for their provinces and the repository of triumphal *insignia*. It was also used for meetings of the Senate when reports of military successes were to be received or the award of triumphs considered.[20] Tradition required meetings of the Senate to be held in a *templum*, which accounts for the fact that Caesar's assassination took place in a hall attached to the portico of Pompey's theatre; for that building was a *templum* of Venus Victrix, of which the *aedes* was approached by the steps of the *cavea* (cf. p. 101 below). Temples were also often used as safe deposits: the ancient Temple of Saturn housed the *aerarium*, the State treasury; and Juvenal refers[21] to an incident when thieves broke into the Temple of Mars Ultor and stole property from it, so that people decided that Castor was a more reliable guardian. The Temple of Juno Moneta on the Capitoline hill housed the mint.

Two later Augustan temples are also important enough to be mentioned, both replacements for much older ones in the Forum Romanum and both dedicated by Augustus' son-in-law and successor Tiberius: the peripteral Temple of Castor and Pollux (dedicated A.D. 6), of which three columns with their entablature still stand on the massive podium (pl. 7); and the Temple of Concord (A.D. 10), on a restricted site below the slope of the Capitoline hill which necessitated an unusual plan, with a six-column

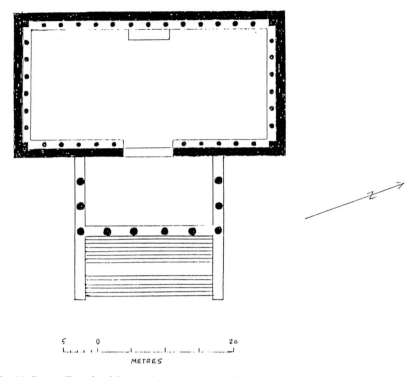

Fig. 29: Rome, Temple of Concord: restored plan. The detailed arrangements are largely conjectural.

(hexastyle) porch projecting from a rectangular cella whose long axis was at right angles to that of the porch (fig. 29). The Temple of Castor (usually so called in common parlance) in addition to its function as a safe deposit also seems to have served as the office of the consuls and had formerly been used for meetings of the Senate;[22] since Cicero's time the Temple of Concord had more frequently been used for this purpose, and certainly its unusual plan must have made it a particularly convenient council chamber. These two temples show the full development of the Roman Corinthian order, with richly decorated capitals and elaborate mouldings on architrave and cornice (contrasting with the frieze, which is still plain); the modillions of the cornice are now developed to a full double scroll, and alternate with coffered soffit panels each containing a rosette. This version of the Corinthian order, worked out by the architects of Augustan Rome, was

to spread throughout the Roman Empire, not only in the architecture of
temples but wherever (especially in interiors) architectural embellishment
was required in the great enclosed spaces made possible by new methods of
construction. The elements of the order were retained for their traditional
associations and decorative value, even though such buildings structurally
had nothing in common with the simple post-and-lintel which had been
the basis of Greek architectural practice. Roman Corinthian was also, of
course, the inspiration for much of the architectural development of the
Renaissance from the fifteenth century onwards.

It was not only in the city of Rome that temples were erected to cel-
ebrate the establishment of the new régime; and no doubt in the towns of
Italy and the provinces they served a similar range of functions to the temples in Rome. One of the best preserved of all Roman temples is the Maison
Carrée, at Nîmes in southern France, the Roman colony of Nemausus in
Gallia Narbonensis. Until recently it was thought to have been built by M.
Agrippa and dedicated in 16 B.C.; but re-examination[23] of the holes on the
frieze left by the fastenings of the bronze letters of the dedicatory inscription has shown that the supposed evidence for this is illusory, and that the
original and only inscription was in honour of Agrippa's sons Gaius and
Lucius, whom Augustus had adopted as his heirs with the title *principes
iuventutis* 'leaders of the youth'. The date should therefore be that indicated by the inscription, A.D. 1/2. This building (pl. 17) is much smaller
than the great Augustan temples in Rome (12.29 x 25.13m). It faced on
to the Forum of the colony, and is approached by a broad flight of steps
between walls which are extensions of the sides of the podium. The façade
has six Corinthian columns, and two columns return on the flanks to form
the entrance porch. As in the late Republican Temple of Portunus (above,
pp. 72f), the colonnade is continued as half-columns engaged in the wall
of the cella along the flanks and round the back, making the temple pseudoperipteral, six columns by eleven—the standard Hellenistic ratio. The
Corinthian capitals resemble those of the Temple of Mars Ultor, and the
frieze is decorated with scrolls of acanthus foliage which recall the decoration of the screen walls of the Ara Pacis. Given the official nature of this
monument, it is not impossible that craftsmen were brought from Rome to
work on it.

Besides the pseudoperipteral plan, another feature which the Maison
Carrée shares with the Temple of Portunus is its unusual orientation, facing
north; and this may be an appropriate place to say something about the
orientation of Roman temples. The great majority of Greek temples face
east: that is to say, their entrance door is at the east end, and the cult
statue is placed against, or in front of, the western wall of the cella. In

practice 'east' seems to have meant the direction of sunrise on the day of the temple's foundation or the principal feast day of the divinity concerned; thus on that day the rays of the rising sun would shine through the open door of the cella and strike the god's image. This is presumably what Vitruvius means when he says 'let the altars look to the east',[24] since, as we have seen, the altar was regularly placed in the open in front of the entrance of the building. In Italian practice, however, there seems to have been no fixed rule for orientation. What originally determined the direction of a temple was, as indicated in the definitions with which we began this chapter, the area of sky indicated by the augur for the taking of auspices. The Capitoline temple faced south, as did the original senate house, the Curia Hostilia in the Forum Romanum, which as we have seen (pp. 40, 79) must have been inaugurated as a *templum*;[25] in early times south was the traditional direction for an augur to face the sky. But in later practice Roman temples are found facing in almost any direction, though there is a distinct preference for the arc from north-east through south to north-west. The Forum Romanum, for example, whose longitudinal axis runs approximately NW-SE, has temples facing on to it from all four sides; and in the case of the imperial Fora orientation seems to have been determined by town-planning requirements. Similar considerations probably account for the northward direction of the Maison Carrée.

Temples either of the imperial cult or of other official cults (including Capitolia) were erected in many cities of Italy and the provinces during the Augustan and Julio-Claudian periods; many more must have existed than are known today. Even from those of which remains are extant, it is clear that there was much variety in plan and design. At Ostia a small prostyle temple of Rome and Augustus was built at the south-east end of the newly laid-out Forum, facing the Capitolium (itself either late Republican or Augustan); the latter was replaced by a much grander building when the Forum was enlarged in the time of Hadrian. At Pola (Pula) in Istria a pair of small temples flanked a larger central one on the north side of the Forum: the western (and better preserved) one of the pair was built between A.D. 2 and 14 and dedicated to Rome and Augustus. At Aosta, the Augustan colony of Augusta Praetoria in north Italy, a temple stood off centre in the middle of a precinct surrounded by a double colonnade—a surprising piece of asymmetry in a plan which is otherwise laid out with military precision (cf. fig. 6). Vienna (Vienne) in Gaul and Barcino (Barcelona) in Spain were other places which had temples similar to the Maison Carrée, but the former was peripteral *sine postico* and the latter apparently fully peripteral; both were temples of Rome and Augustus, though the one at Vienne was rededicated to Augustus and Livia, presumably in A.D. 42 when Claudius

Plate 1: Aerial view of Pompeii, looking east. The Forum is in the foreground to right; the theatre complex can be seen above the southern (right) end of the Forum. (F.U. 28553 F)

Plate 2: Aerial view of Lepcis Magna, looking north. In the foreground, the Hadrianic Baths; in middle distance, left of centre, the Severan Forum and Basilica, with the Old Forum beyond; on the right of the picture, Wadi Lebda running down to the harbour. (The British School at Rome)

Plate 3: Perge: water channel in centre of street. (E. J. Owens)

Plate 4: Gerasa: colonnaded street. (A. J. Brothers)

Plate 5: Cosa: aerial view of north-east corner of Forum, showing entrance, atrium, basilica, curia and comitium (F.U. 14164 F).

Plate 6: Rome: oblique aerial view of Forum Romanum, looking north-west. At the far end, the Tabularium (with later structures built on top); on left side, Temple of Saturn, Basilica Iulia, Temple of Castor; on right side, Curia (senate house) and Basilica Paulli. (F.U. 14874 F)

Plate 7: Rome, Forum Romanum, looking north. In foreground, Temple of Castor, with Basilica Iulia beyond; on extreme right, Curia; in background, Tabularium. (F.U. 10872)

Plate 8: Pompeii: the Basilica, looking towards the tribunal. (A. J. Brothers)

Plate 9:   Rome, Basilica Paulli. Drawing by Giuliano da Sangallo, *c*.1500. (F.U. 12204 F)

Plate 10: Rome, Basilica Ulpia. Restored drawing of interior. (F.U. 12263 F)

Plate 11: Rome, Trajan's Market: interior of hall. (I. M. Barton)

Plate 12:   Trier, Basilica of Constantine, west side. (F.U. 9140 F)

Plate 13:   Ephesus, Library of Celsus: façade. (W. H. Manning)

Plate 14: Rome, Forum Boarium: Republican temples. Left, round temple of (?)Hercules Victor; right, temple of Portunus. (I. M. Barton)

Plate 15:   Cori, Temple of Hercules. (F.U. 19769)

Plate 16: Rome, Temple of Mars Ultor. (I. M. Barton)

Plate 17: Nemausus, Augustan temple ('Maison Carrée'). (A. J. Brothers)

Plate 18: Heliopolis (Baalbek), Temple of Jupiter Heliopolitanus. In foreground, part of the temple of Bacchus. (F.U. 9009 F)

Plate 19: Thugga, Capitolium. (I. M. Barton)

Plate 20: Sufetula, group of three temples (?Capitolium). (I. M. Barton)

Plate 21: Rome, Pantheon. Painting of the interior by G. P. Pannini, before c.1740. (Statens Museum for Kunst, København)

Plate 22: Bostra, theatre: cavea and orchestra. (A. J. Brothers)

Plate 23: Arausio, theatre: *scaenae frons*. (A. J. Brothers)

Plate 24: Arausio, theatre: rear wall of *scaena*. (A. J. Brothers)

Plate 25: Pompeii, amphitheatre. (A. J. Brothers)

Plate 26: Nemausus, amphitheatre: exterior. (A. J. Brothers)

Plate 27: Nemausus, amphitheatre: interior. (A. J. Brothers)

Plate 28: Puteoli, amphitheatre: substructures. (A. J. Brothers)

Plate 29: Rome, Circus of Maxentius, aerial view. (F.U. 4793 F)

Plate 30: Cologne, the Eifel aqueduct. A typical stretch of subterranean aqueduct, with inspection manhole in the foreground, uncovered during road-building. (K. Grewe, Rheinisches Amt für Bodendenkmalpflege)

Plate 31: Lyon, the Gier aqueduct: *venter* bridge at bottom of the Beaunant siphon. The great width of the bridge, carrying a battery of nine lead pipes laid side by side, and its shallow superstructure, lacking the usual masonry conduit, are clearly visible. (A. T. Hodge)

Plate 32: The Pont du Gard, carrying the Roman aqueduct of Nemausus (Nîmes). The highest of all Roman bridges (50m), it was built about 19 B.C., probably by Agrippa. (A. J. Brothers)

Plate 33: The aqueduct of Segovia. (Spanish National Tourist Office)

Plate 34: Aspendos, aqueduct: one of the so-called 'pressure towers'. (K. R. Hopwood)

Plate 35: Rome, Aqua Marcia. Model of the Ponte Lupo. This was the greatest aqueduct bridge on the metropolitan water system. (Museo della Civiltà romana)

Plate 36: Rome, Aqua Claudia: the arcade carrying the aqueduct across the Campagna. The conduit of the Anio Novus was later added on top. (A. T. Hodge)

Plate 37: Rome, Aqua Claudia: arcade with brick liner added, to strengthen the arches and seal leaks. (A. T. Hodge)

Plate 38: Rome, Porta Maggiore. The point at which all the eastern aqueducts entered the city together. The channels of the Aqua Claudia and, above, the Anio Novus are clearly seen. (A. T. Hodge)

Plate 39: Nemausus, *castellum divisorium*. (A. J. Brothers)

Plate 40: Montpellier (France): eighteenth-century *château d'eau* du Peyrou. (A. T. Hodge)

deified his grandmother.[26]

The transformation of cities in north Africa and the Greek East which was described in the first chapter (pp. 21ff.) included the provision of temples of Roman type. At Lepcis Magna the north-west side of the Old Forum (fig. 21) was occupied by a row of three temples, all peripteral *sine postico*: on the left was the earliest, probably pre-Augustan, a temple of Liber Pater (the Latin name for a Punic deity identified with Dionysus); its peristyle was almost square in plan, with a side of about 20m. The next, at the right-hand end of the row, was a smaller temple of unknown dedication, which was built about the middle of the Augustan period. Finally in the centre, and connected to the Temple of Liber Pater by a bridge between the fronts of the podia, stood the largest of the three, the Temple of Rome and Augustus, which was started after Augustus' death and dedicated in A.D. 19. It has a feature which is found in several north African temples: the front of the podium is extended well forward of the columns of the façade and ends in a sheer wall rising from the pavement of the Forum, with small flights of steps on either side. This feature appears to have originated in Italy, where the earliest known example is in the rebuilt Capitolium at Pompeii (c.80 B.C.; above, p. 75). Variations of it are to be found in three Augustan temples in Rome: those of Venus Genetrix, Divus Iulius and Castor. There is no doubt that the purpose of this arrangement was to provide a platform from which orators could address the people gathered in the Forum. This is explicit in the Temple of Divus Iulius, where the beaks (*rostra*) of ships captured at the Battle of Actium (31 B.C.) were displayed directly opposite the Republican speakers' platform, known as the Rostra because the ships' beaks captured at Antium (338 B.C.) were fixed to its front. Suetonius records[27] that Augustus received two funeral eulogies, one spoken in front of the Temple of Divus Iulius (*pro aede divi Iuli*) by Tiberius, the other from the old *Rostra* by Tiberius' son Drusus. The presence of carved *rostra* on the front of the podium of the Lepcis temple shows that the intention there was the same.

Even in Greek lands temples of Roman type are commonly found. Corinth had a row of six small prostyle temples on podia at the west end of its Agora, two of which belong to the Augustan period. At Antioch in Pisidia, the temple of Augustus and Mên (a local deity) stands in the middle of a semicircular portico with a monumental axial approach, and though the workmanship is Greek, the ornamentation is very similar to that of Augustan buildings in Rome. It should, however, be remembered that both Corinth and Antioch were refounded as Roman colonies, in 44 and 25 B.C. (or soon after) respectively; elsewhere older traditions continued. At Athens the Temple of Rome and Augustus (27 B.C.) was a little circular building without a cella, having nine Ionic columns closely modelled on the nearby Erechtheum. In Asia Minor temples of Hellenistic type were still being built in the second century A.D.; even the Temple of Rome and Augustus at Ancyra in Galatia (Ankara), famous for the text of Augustus' *Res Gestae* which is inscribed on its walls, was so conventional in plan and design that some have dated it to the second century B.C.

One of the most ambitious architectural undertakings of this period was the provision of a new Romanised sanctuary at Heliopolis (Baalbek in Lebanon), where an ancient cult centre going back at least to the sixth century B.C. had been rebuilt in the Hellenistic era. Soon after the foundation of a Roman colony there in 16 B.C. plans were made for a much enlarged complex which, it has been suggested by Ward-Perkins, was officially intended 'to serve as a focus for the religious loyalties of central Syria'.[28] Rather than promote the cult of Rome and Augustus, it was decided here to exploit the pre-existing cult and to develop the sanctuary on a grandiose scale as an advertisement for Roman power and wealth. The design incorporated both Roman and Hellenistic features as well as some derived from oriental tradition (fig. 30). Roman was the monumental axiality of the whole scheme and the raising of the principal temple (of Jupiter Heliopolitanus) on a high podium approached by a broad flight of steps at the front; Greek the peripteral plan of the temple, with ten columns on the façdes and nineteen on the flanks (again the standard Hellenistic proportion). The side and rear walls of the cella and the columns of the front porch seem to have been in line with the third column from the corner of the colonnade; this type of plan, called pseudodipteral, was a favourite with Hellenistic architects (it is also found in the temple at Ancyra). The dimensions of the temple were colossal. It was not indeed the largest temple of classical antiquity: that distinction belonged to the Temple of Artemis at Ephesus, whose dimensions on the stylobate were 55 x 109m, compared with 48 x 88m for the Baalbek temple, which is still larger than any previous Roman temple (pl. 18). What was exceptional was its height: mounted on a podium 13.5m high, the columns rise to a height of nearly 20m. Including the entablature and pediment, the façade of the temple must have towered almost 44m above the pavement of the courtyard in front. The column shafts are unfluted, unusually for temple architecture in this period. The design of the Corinthian capitals and parts of the entablature can be compared with Augustan temples in Rome, but the temple was a long time building (it was still unfinished in A.D. 60) and there were changes in design as the work progressed. A quite un-Roman feature is the frieze, in which the foreparts of bulls and lions alternately are mounted on projecting brackets, in allusion to the Syrian deities identified

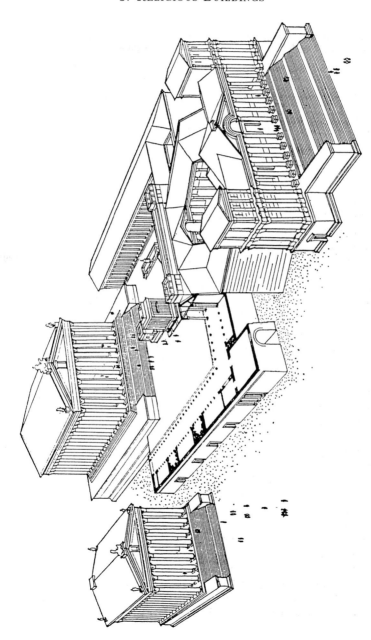

Fig. 30: Baalbeck, Sanctuary of Jupiter Heliopolitanus: restored axonometric view.

respectively with Jupiter (Ba'al) and Venus (Atargatis); the origin of this device is perhaps to be found in Persian architecture. Even when the main temple was finished, work continued on the sanctuary for at least another century and a half: the adjacent Temple of Bacchus, smaller but similar in plan and even more richly decorated, particularly inside the cella, was built in the first half of the second century A.D.; the series of courts leading to the Temple of Jupiter was being built throughout the second century, and was not completed till some time in the third with the huge screen surrounding the entrance gateway.

Space does not permit discussion of other, equally interesting, eastern temples, such as Herod's Temple of Rome and Augustus at Samaria, the Temple of Artemis at Gerasa (Jerash) (cf. pp. 26ff) or the Temple of Augustus at Philae in upper Egypt, all of which were more or less classical in plan and design. Still further east, at such sites as Si' in the Hauran (southern Syria), Palmyra in the Syrian desert (cf. pp. 28f) and Dura-Europos on the Euphrates, are temples which, although they use many of the ornaments of classical architecture, essentially belong to a different tradition.

It is time to return to Rome and the western provinces, and to consider some of the developments of the period from Claudius to Trajan. The classical temple was introduced to the newly-conquered province of Britain when it was decided to found a temple of Claudius at the new colony of Camulodunum (Colchester), which according to Tacitus was one of the contributory causes of the revolt of Boudicca, since the Britons regarded it 'as a citadel of permanent domination' (*quasi arx aeternae dominationis*).[29] The massive podium still exists under Colchester castle, and although nothing of the superstructure survives it is clear that it was of typical Roman plan and comparable in size with the Temple of Venus Genetrix (above, p. 78); thus it was considerably larger than any of the known Augustan temples in the western provinces. Most of the larger cities in Gaul and Britain probably had at least one temple of classical type: impressive examples are known to have existed at Narbo (Narbonne: the Capitolium, perhaps rebuilt after a fire in A.D. 145), Aventicum (Avenches in Switzerland) and Verulamium. The commonest type of religious structure in these provinces, however, had quite a different plan: a square (occasionally polygonal or circular) cella, often rising two stories, surrounded by a veranda. These 'Romano-Celtic' temples—originally of timber, later of stone or brick—are to be found not only in towns (e.g. Autun, Périgueux, Caerwent) but also often in sanctuaries in the countryside, where they were no doubt the centres of traditional pre-Roman cults. Few of them were affected by the introduction of classical patterns into their countries, and even where elements of classical design were incorporated the effect was usually different from that of a standard

Roman temple: the Temple of Lenus-Mars at Augusta Treverorum (Trier), reconstructed on classicising lines in the third century, is a good example (fig. 31).

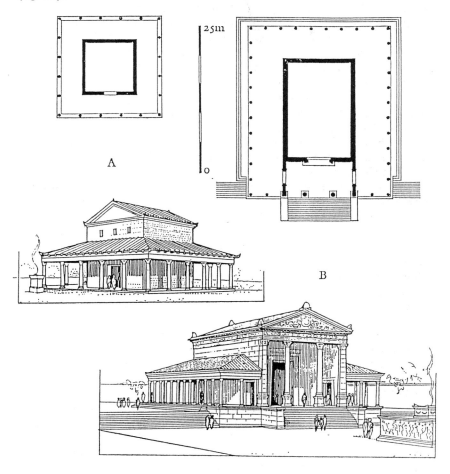

Fig. 31: Trier, Romano-Celtic Temples: (A) Temple 38, a typical Romano-Celtic plan; (B) Temple of Lenus-Mars, in its latest, classicising form, third century A.D.

In general the half-century following Augustus' death in A.D. 14 saw few new developments, no doubt because most cities by then had already built the new temples they needed; but under Nero and the Flavian emper-

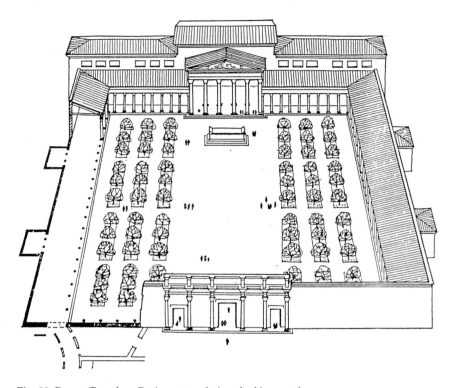

Fig. 32: Rome, Templum Pacis: restored view, looking south-east.

ors in the last forty years of the first century A.D. some bold experiments were tried. Vespasian created the first addition to the imperial Fora in Rome when he converted the site of the former meat-market (*macellum*), which had recently been removed to a new position, into a great monument to commemorate his victory in civil war and his conquest of Judaea, the Temple of Peace (Templum Pacis). The similarity of its plan to that of market buildings like the one at Pompeii (cf. p. 60) suggests that the original layout was retained at least in part (fig. 32). The *templum* consisted of a rectangular enclosure, 110 x 135m, surrounded by porticoes and laid out as a formal garden. Behind the portico on the south-east side, facing the entrance, was a range of buildings in the centre of which, its six façade columns ranged with the colonnade, stood the *aedes* with an almost square cella terminating in an apse. We can get an idea of the appearance of

this building from the surviving columns and entablature of the Temple of
Vespasian at the north-west end of the Forum Romanum. Adjoining the
Temple of Concord (above, pp. 79f) on a similarly restricted site, it had
a cella of which the breadth exceeded the length, and for the same reason
the steps of the podium were set between the six Corinthian columns of the
façade. The rich decoration of the entablature shows the Roman style of
architectural ornament at its peak of excellence. Another example of fine
ornament from this period is the rebuilt Temple of Venus Genetrix, dedicated by Trajan in 113 but perhaps begun under Domitian. It was probably
one of a number of buildings which are known to have been severely damaged by a fire in 80, and its superstructure seems to have been entirely new
on the original podium.

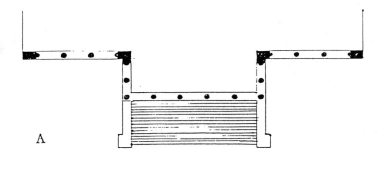

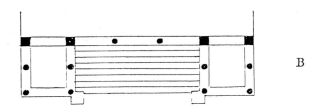

Fig. 33: Sketch plans (not to scale) of façade arrangements: (a) Capitolium at Brescia;
(b) temple at Trieste.

The adventurous planning of this period is to be seen in two temples in northern Italy, at Tergeste (Trieste) and Brixia (Brescia), each of which was probably the Capitolium of its city, though positive identification is lacking (fig. 33). The Tergeste temple, which was later converted into a Christian church, had broad projections of the podium on either side of the central stairway; each carried two pairs of columns and two columns stood at the head of the stairs, so that the whole gave the appearance of a hexastyle façade. An inscription[30] records that it was the gift of a prefect of the fleet named Claudius Quirinalis, presumably the man whose enforced suicide Tacitus records under the year 56;[31] the building must therefore have been completed by then. The Brixia temple was dedicated in 73. It too has a tripartite division of the façade, but in this case it is the central part, with six columns, which projects in front of side wings, each of which has two columns between pilasters. This division corresponds with three cellas behind, making it virtually certain that this temple was for the Capitoline cult.

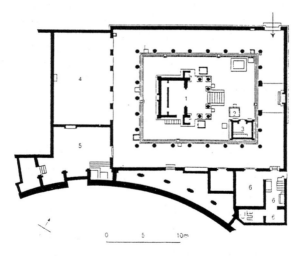

Fig. 34: Pompeii, Temple of Isis: plan. 1. Temple; 2. Main altar; 3. Building with water tank; 4. Meeting hall; 5. Initiation chamber; 6. Priests' lodging.

Unusual planning is also to be seen in temples at Pompeii which had been built (or rebuilt) after the earthquake of 62 before the final destruction of the town by the eruption of Vesuvius in 79. The Temple of Isis (fig. 34), destroyed by the earthquake, was completely rebuilt at the expense of a

wealthy freedman, who thus obtained entry for his six-year-old son into the
town council (*ordo decurionum*), from which he himself was debarred by
his status.[32] The peculiarities of its plan are no doubt to be explained by
the special requirements of the cult. Immediately after the earthquake a
shrine to the Lares was built on the east side of the Forum (fig. 14) as a
propitiatory offering; it consisted of an irregularly shaped but symmetrical
enclosure open to the Forum, with an apsidal exedra at the far end. Next
to it in the 70s was built the Temple of Vespasian, in which the *aedes* was
a very small building on a podium with steps only at the sides, which was
placed against the rear wall of a rectangular enclosure.

Few buildings in the provinces can be certainly assigned to the Flavian
period, but with the second century A.D. we reach the period of most rapid
and widespread development in the cities of the Empire, particularly under
Hadrian (117–138) and his Antonine successors (138–192). The practice of
individual citizens endowing their towns with public buildings, of which we
have seen examples at Tergeste and Pompeii, is of course derived from the
Roman Republican tradition and can be traced in provincial cities from the
time of Augustus (e.g. the buildings at Lepcis mentioned in the last chapter, pp. 59ff). In the second century it became a positive flood, and even
buildings which we might have expected to be undertaken by the municipal authorities were often erected by private initiative. The building of a
temple for the Capitoline cult in some cases at least marked the attainment
of civic status as *municipium* or *colonia*, but even so in Africa, where the
evidence is most abundant, out of some twenty Capitolia where relevant
evidence is preserved perhaps half a dozen were paid for by the munificence
of individuals, either in their lifetime or by testamentary bequest. The best
known and best preserved of these is the one at Thugga (Dougga), erected
between 166 and 169, which may be taken as fairly typical of the smaller
classical temples of Africa (it is comparable in size to the Maison Carrée,
about 13 x 22 m). It stands on high ground overlooking the streets of the
town (pl. 19), and is raised on a podium about 2m high whose side walls
are, as usual, prolonged to flank the stairs. The podium contains a crypt
which was divided into three by two longitudinal arcades, an arrangement
which is quite often found inside podia. The façade is of four Corinthian
columns, about 8m high, with a return of one column. The cella walls were
rendered in stucco, with moulded pilasters and entablature continuing the
line of the order of the porch. Inside the cella the back wall contained three
niches for the cult statues.

As an example of a large temple, comparable to the Temple of Venus
Genetrix at Rome, we may take the Capitolium of Thamugadi (Timgad).
The original layout of the *colonia* (cf. p. 22) contained no place for a Capi-

tolium, the only temple being a small one inconspicuously sited on one side of the Forum, but still having the front of its podium adapted as a speakers' platform. When the Capitolium came to be built c.160, it was placed outside the original area and at an angle of about fifteen degrees to the original street grid. Everything about the temple was on a large scale, though even so the lost Capitolium of Carthage probably surpassed it in size. The podium (23 x 35m) was nearly 6m high, and was approached by no fewer than thirty-eight steps, divided into two flights; its interior was divided into three longitudinal vaulted chambers under the cella and a single transverse vault under the porch. The plan of the temple was peripteral *sine postico*; the Corinthian columns, two of which have been re-erected, are some 14m high, and the entablature was richly decorated.

One other African Capitolium calls for mention, and that is the group of three temples which in all probability formed the Capitolium of Sufetula (Sbeïtla). They stand at the west end of an enclosure whose entrance gateway bears dedications to Antoninus Pius and his adopted sons; their titles date it between 140 and 144. The temples were obviously planned as a group (pl. 20), since the central one has no stairway; its podium, which is rather over 3m high, has a sheer front, no doubt to serve as a platform for orators (cf. p. 83), and the approach to it was by bridges from the porches of the side temples. A much earlier example of such an arrangement existed at Lepcis (p. 83 above), but here it should perhaps be seen as a development from triple temples like the one at Brixia (p. 90). It was not, so far as our knowledge goes, very commonly adopted: the only other example known is at Baelo (Bolonia) in Spain. All three temples were prostyle, with four-column façades: the central one had Composite capitals (a combination of Ionic and Corinthian features first known from the Arch of Titus in Rome) and was pseudoperipteral; the others had Corinthian columns whose line was continued by pilasters along the side and rear walls of the cella.

In Africa, as in other parts of the Empire, local traditions continued, affected to a greater or less degree by the adoption of classical conventions. A characteristic type of sanctuary is one which has a row of three small chambers occupying the whole or most of one side of an enclosure. This is distinct from the Roman Capitolium plan, with which it has nothing in common except the triple cella; it lacks the high podium and impressive façade, and tends to form a self-contained enclosure rather than to be part of a larger architectural design. The type is best exemplified at Thugga, where no fewer than three temples apart from the Capitolium have a triple arrangement of shrines; they are dedicated to Mercury, Tellus and Saturn, the last of these being dated to A.D. 195 and succeeding an earlier sanctuary of the Punic Ba'al on the same site. In each case the three chambers occupy the whole of one side of a courtyard and are entered directly from it. Although some of the architectural details of temples like these are derived from the classical tradition, they seem likely to belong essentially to a Punic tradition of religious building, just as the 'Romano-Celtic' temples of Gaul and Britain do to a Celtic one. Both categories indicate the extent to which, in religious matters at least, Romanisation in parts of the Empire was only skin-deep and brought little significant change to traditional ways: to a German Mars was still Lenus, to an African Saturn was still Ba'al.

Meanwhile the pace of new building in the capital continued unabated. A huge new temple in honour of the deified Trajan was built beyond the Basilica Ulpia (above, p. 55) and finished off the mighty complex of the imperial Fora (fig. 17). Hadrian in turn was commemorated by a temple in the Campus Martius, usually called the Hadrianeum, which is of interest for its use of a vaulted ceiling in the cella in place of the traditional timber roofing; and his successor Antoninus Pius built a conventional hexastyle temple in the Forum Romanum to his wife Faustina, who died in 141. But the most important and innovative temples were both due to Hadrian's own passionate interest in architectural problems: the Pantheon and the Temple of Venus and Rome.

Stamps on bricks used in the structure of the Pantheon make it certain that it was constructed during the reign of Hadrian, between c.118 and c.128, although the inscription on the frieze of the entrance porch refers to its predecessor, built by Agrippa and dedicated in 25 B.C., which had been destroyed in the fire of A.D. 80.[33] Excavation beneath the porch in the 1890s revealed the foundations of an earlier rectangular building (c.19 x 42m), which is generally assumed to have been Agrippa's Pantheon. This building had a porch facing south across a paved area towards the Baths of Agrippa. The rebuilding recorded as having been undertaken by Domitian perhaps retained the original plan, but this temple in turn was burnt in a fire started by lightning in 110, and when Hadrian came to rebuild it he decided on a bold new design (fig. 35). The site of the original Pantheon was occupied by a new north-facing entrance porch with eight columns on the façade. These columns have monolithic unfluted shafts of Egyptian granite, with marble bases and Corinthian capitals. Columns returning behind the third and sixth façade columns divide the porch into three: the side sections terminate in niches which apparently held statues of Augustus and Agrippa; the central one leads to the doorway of the great rotunda which is the cella of Hadrian's Pantheon. The awkwardness of the join between the rectangular porch and the circular cella has often been criticised; but it must be remembered that only the façade would have been visible from ground level in antiquity. From the courtyard outside, the building would

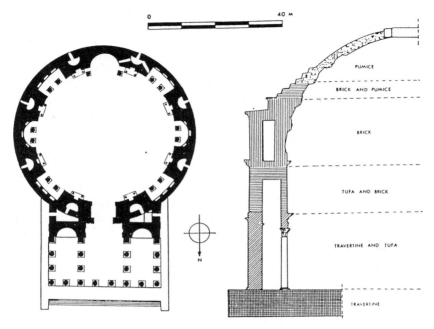

Fig. 35: Rome, Pantheon: plan and section showing filling materials.

have appeared to be a conventional octastyle temple, and when passing through the porch and the doorway the visitor would have been unaware of the presence of a transitional structure on either side and overhead. Once he got inside, the magnificent boldness of the design would—as it still does—command such admiration as to exclude criticism.

For the rotunda—the great triumph of Hadrianic, and arguably of all Roman, architecture—is not just another round temple like those mentioned above (p. 73), though the existence of such buildings may have been one part of the inspiration for the idea of the Pantheon. Its architectural ancestry is to be found in secular buildings—the domed circular halls of bath-buildings (e.g. at Pompeii and Baiae, cf. p. 49) and octagonal rooms in palaces like Nero's Golden House and Domitian's on the Palatine, in which the interior is lighted by a circular opening (*oculus*) at the top of the dome. The construction of such halls was made possible by the skill of Roman builders in the use of concrete with relieving arches of brick. Even so, the mighty dome of the Pantheon, 43.2m in diameter, was more than twice the span of anything attempted hitherto and was not surpassed even in the

Renaissance (Michelangelo's dome of St Peter's has a diameter of 42.5m). Like the great bath-buildings discussed in chapter 2, it is an architecture of the interior. The external appearance is irrelevant: what is important is the organisation of internal space. Despite some minor alterations since antiquity, the interior of the Pantheon (pl. 21) still conveys essentially the impression intended by its architect. The rhythm of its alternating piers and niches, the harmony of its proportions and the restrained elegance of its decoration make it one of the most satisfying interiors ever created.

The Temple of Venus and Rome, completed in A.D. 135, was a bold attempt to recreate the Greek classical temple in Roman terms. It was on the scale of the great sixth-century B.C. temples of Ionia and stood centrally in a colonnaded enclosure, raised on a low stepped platform in the Greek manner. Its stylobate was a double square (52.5 x 105m), it was completely peripteral (ten by twenty columns) and there were two cellas back to back, one for each of the goddesses, of identical size. Details are uncertain, because the surviving superstructure belongs to a reconstruction of the early fourth century; but the vaulted ceilings may, as in the Hadrianeum, be an original feature. The building was criticised at the time for its unsatisfactory proportions: a Greek temple needed more clear space around it for viewing, and a building of Roman proportions needed to be raised on a higher podium (as at Baalbek). It is perhaps not surprising that Hadrian's successors reverted to more conventional plans.

Although new temples continued to be built, especially, as we have seen, in the provinces, architectural innovators turned to other types of building. Temple architecture became for the most part lifeless and repetitive, apart from an occasional *jeu d'esprit* like the charming little round temple of Venus at Baalbek, which is probably of the first half of the third century. What the architecture of pagan temples had come to by the fourth century is illustrated by the last reconstruction (c.320) of the ancient Temple of Saturn in the Forum Romanum, where feeble four-sided Ionic capitals and a poorly-proportioned entablature surmount graceless unfluted columns. The advent of Christianity came none too soon to reinvigorate the religious architecture of the Roman Empire.

NOTES

1. Oxford Latin Dictionary, s.v. *templum.*

2. ILS 7213, lines 8, 10 and 23.

3. Livy 2.8: Dionysius of Halicarnassus (4.61) places it in the third year (507).

4. Vitruvius 4.7.

5. 4.7.1.

6. 4.7.4f.

7. 25.40.2.

8. Vitruvius 3.2.5; Velleius Paterculus 1.11.5.

9. 3.2.5.

10. The evidence is discussed in F. Rakob and W.D. Heilmeyer, *Der Rundtempel an Tiber in Rom* (Mainz, 1973), 29; 36ff.

11. Ovid, *Fasti* 6. 261-282.

12. ILS 59.

13. 3.2.5.

14. Plutarch, *Gaius Gracchus* 17.6.

15. Vitruvius 3.3.5; Pliny, *Natural History* 34.57.

16. Plutarch, *Cicero* 33.1; Cicero, *de domo sua* passim, esp. 108; 110-112.

17. restoration: 20.4. building: 19.

18. cf. Horace, *Odes* 3.6.

19. 4.1.2.

20. Suetonius, *Divus Augustus* 29.2; *Caligula* 44.2; Dio Cassius 55.10.2f.

21. 14. 260-2.

22. Several episodes in late Republican history place consular activity in and around this temple: note esp. Cicero, *pro Sestio* 79, where Sestius as tribune goes there to find the consul. For other references, and other examples of temples used as magistrates' offices, see J.E. Stambaugh in ANRW II.16.1 (1978), 582.

23. R. Amy and P. Gros, *La Maison Carrée de Nîmes* (Paris, 1979), 177-94.

24. 4.9.1.

25. Pliny, *Natural History* 7.212: midday was announced when the sun was seen at a specified point from in front of the senate house. For an augur facing south, cf. Livy 1.18.6f.

26. Suetonius, *Divus Claudius* 11.2.

27. *Divus Augustus* 100.3.

28. *Roman Imperial Architecture* (1981), 314.

29. *Annals* 14.31. Another grievance was the enormous sums which the priests were expected to spend *specie religionis* ('on the pretext of religious observance').

30. ILS 2702.

31. *Annals* 13.30.

32. ILS 6367.

33. Dio 53.27.2f; 66.24.1f. On the buildings of Hadrian in Rome, see M.T. Boatwright, *Hadrian and the City of Rome* (Princeton, 1987).

4. Buildings for Entertainment

A.J. BROTHERS

Many people who know little else about the Roman world will have heard
the much-quoted statement that the Roman mob yearned for 'just two
things, bread and circuses';[1] others, recalling seeing *Ben Hur* or *Quo Vadis?*,
will have formed the impression that the Romans' addiction to public entertainment, often of a violent and bloody kind, was as insatiable as that of the
modern football fan. Although, as often, such generalisations need qualifi-
cation, these particular ones are in the main correct. The Romans' entertainments began modestly enough, comparatively early in Rome's history,
with crude performances of drama or near-drama, uncomplicated races and
straightforward fights; but by the time the empire was at its height, these
few simple spectacles had become a bewildering variety of well-organised
events including plays and mimes, recitals and declamations, gladiatorial
contests, animal baiting, mass combat of man against man, man against
beast or beast against beast, mock naval battles, water ballets, athletic
contests and chariot racing. Instead of taking place, as originally, on fairly
few occasions, mainly of a religious nature, they were later held on almost
half the days in the year, at funerals, victories and triumphs, on imperial
birthdays, or in celebration of the dedication of some great building or other
public work, as well as at religious festivals. And instead of being held in
the open or in temporary structures erected for the occasion, they were
staged in a number of different permanent buildings, each designed with

the particular event in mind and elaborated in accordance with prevailing taste. Moreover, this picture, albeit with differences of scale and local variations, was reflected throughout the Roman world, from Africa to Britain and from Syria to Spain.

Familiarity with the buildings used for these entertainments is not entirely due to Hollywood, since the massive character of many of them, particularly theatres and amphitheatres, has ensured their survival, often in a fairly complete form. Moreover, sometimes their very massiveness has meant that in the dark and middle ages they were converted into fortresses (like the theatres at Bosra in Syria and Arelate (Arles) in Provence) or even into shelter for entire communities (as with the amphitheatres at Arles and at Nîmes, also in Provence); it has thus proved comparatively easy in more recent times to remove later accretions and reveal the Roman building. These and other examples have become familiar to the modern tourist, especially in Mediterranean lands, and it is in order to offer more inducements to tourists that the buildings have frequently been 'restored' and are still in use today. Some of the entertainments staged in them, like productions of plays in theatres all over the Roman world or Provençal bullfighting in the amphitheatres of southern France, are akin to those for which the buildings were originally intended; others, such as the elaborate performances of *Aida* or *Turandot* in the amphitheatre of Verona, are not. Nevertheless, whether or not the spectacle accords with its setting, to sit among a vast crowd of spectators watching a performance is to feel strangely close to the Roman world.

I. Theatres

One of the earliest entertainments to be found in the Roman world is drama, and it was the popularity of drama, and of its near relations like mime and pantomime, which led to the evolution of the Roman theatre-building. In Rome and Italy, as in most cultures, the origins of drama are lost in antiquity; as in most cultures too, its history is long and complicated. What is clear is that a number of forms of something approaching drama had been present in Italian life for some time before the first proper plays were staged at Rome shortly after the middle of the third century B.C. These early forms—notably mimes and farces—probably arose spontaneously, but at the same time they clearly drew inspiration from the dramas performed in the Greek colonies of southern Italy and Sicily. In 240 B.C. the first true plays were produced at Rome; they were adaptations of Greek originals, and for the next two centuries such Latin versions of Greek tragedies and comedies continued to be written and staged, together with comedies and historical dramas on native Roman themes. By the end of the republic, however, the Romans' tastes in theatre had begun to move in a different direction. Under the empire, plays such as tragedies were written more and more for recitation at gatherings of the intellectual elite, not for performance, while in the live theatre the old mimes and their more sophisticated cousins, pantomimes, held ever-increasing sway. Such entertainments, along with the occasional addition of an isolated scene from drama performed as a *tour de force*, and with acts like jugglers and clowns, remained hugely popular; and outside Rome at least, particularly in the Greek half of the empire, drama retained some of its old attraction. Hence, all over the Roman world, every sizeable town had at least one theatre, and these were frequently enlarged, modernised or adapted to the changing fashions in theatrical entertainment, and were kept in good repair until the end of the Roman world.

Since early Roman drama was so heavily indebted to Greece, it is hardly surprising that the design of Roman theatres was greatly influenced by the design of Greek ones—especially when it is remembered that Romans must have become familiar with the theatres in cities of the Greek West (as, for example, in Sicily) long before they conquered Greece herself. In this connection, for instance, it cannot but be significant that the earliest permanent stone-built theatre in Rome itself, that of Pompey the Great begun in 55 B.C., is specifically said[2] to have been based on the Greek theatre at Mitylene on the Aegean island of Lesbos. But if there are great similarities between Greek and Roman theatres, there are also significant differences. It is probable that many factors combined to bring about the changes which the Romans made to the Greek design: the form of the primitive temporary wooden theatres erected in Rome in the early days obviously played a part, as did the changed character of the dramatic performances themselves in the Roman world; the Roman love of enclosure and of elaborate decoration was also significant, as was their habit of viewing their buildings as interiors rather than stressing their outward appearance; and it was similarly important that the Romans, in contrast to the Greeks, readily exploited the arch and the vault in their constructional techniques and methods.

It should, therefore, be comparatively easy to distinguish a Roman theatre from a Greek one; the two most complete Roman theatres, at Arausio (Orange) in Provence and at Aspendos in Pamphylia (southern Turkey), are as distinctively Roman as the one at Epidauros in the Peloponnese is purely Greek (fig. 36). But sometimes it is not that simple to make the distinction; quite apart from the fact that some theatres are in a very ruined state, others—the large theatre at Pompeii and the theatre at Eph-

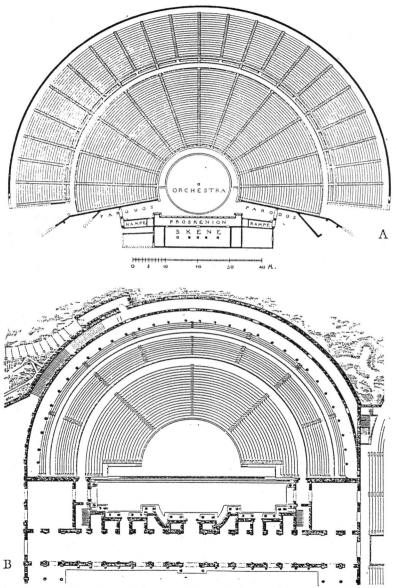

Fig. 36: Comparative plans of Greek and Roman theatres (not to same scale): (a) Epidaurus, fourth century B.C.; (b) Arausio (Orange), first century A.D.

esus are good examples—were originally built in the Greek style, but later 'Romanised' to differing extents. Nor is it possible to make a simple distinction by location, with Roman theatres in the West and Greek in the East; Greek theatres in Sicily and a Roman one in Turkey have already been mentioned, and there are also good examples of Roman theatres in Syria (Bosra, Palmyra), Jordan (Amman, Jerash and Petra), and even, in the form of the theatre of Herodes Atticus, on the slopes of the Athenian acropolis itself. Type, not location, is the key.

Unfortunately, it is not possible to be precise about how and when the typically Roman theatre-design evolved, though it is fairly obvious where it happened. It took place, as might be expected, in Rome and the surrounding areas of southern Italy, and, once the design had been established there, it spread to all parts of the empire. But the stages by which the design emerged can only be guessed at. This is mainly because all theatres built at Rome itself prior to Pompey's theatre of 55 B.C. were temporary, and were demolished after the conclusion of the festival for which they were erected. Such action was taken because the Roman authorities feared that the tough Roman character would become effeminate if it became too accustomed to such new-fangled, 'soft' pursuits. Indeed, we hear[3] that in 154 B.C. a permanent theatre which the censors had started to erect was demolished by senatorial decree on a motion by the staunch traditionalist P. Scipio Nasica. Even a century later, it is hinted,[4] Pompey only got away with the erection of the first permanent theatre through the legal fiction of maintaining that its seats were really no more than the steps of a monumental approach to his temple of Venus Victrix, which stood in the centre at the back of the auditorium (cf. p. 79). Roman writers mention some of the earlier temporary structures: the elder Pliny, for example,[5] was clearly scandalised by the extravagant decoration of the magnificent example erected by M. Aemilius Scaurus in 58 B.C. It is clear from his description that these temporary buildings were becoming increasingly elaborate, and Tacitus[6] remarks that in the end it was regarded as more economical to build a permanent theatre than to go to the expense of erecting and demolishing these costly temporary ones year after year. It is interesting to note that outside Rome, notably in Latium and Campania, permanent theatres were being built before 55 B.C., partly perhaps because such areas were sufficiently far removed from the vigilance of the Roman authorities, and partly because, as with the large theatre at Pompeii in its early form, Greek influence was strong. Several of these, as at Gabii, Pietrabbondante, Tivoli and Praeneste—in keeping with the religious nature of the occasions on which plays were performed at this time, and significantly in view of Pompey's later legal fiction at Rome—were associated with religious sanctuaries (cf. p. 73). But at least one was not, the small theatre or *odeum* erected in Pompeii immediately after the foundation of the Sullan colony in the town in 80 B.C. (fig. 37), and this one was built to a typically Roman design. If, then, a 'Roman' theatre could be erected at Pompeii twenty-five years before Pompey's at Rome, it is likely that the temporary ones put up in the capital before Pompey's were also of Roman design; and, in some points at least, Pliny's description of Scaurus' theatre seems to confirm this.

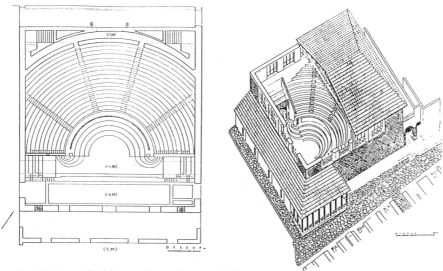

Fig. 37: Pompeii, Odeum: plan and restored view

The design, then, must have emerged no later than the early first century B.C. It combined the Greek idea of a curved, sloping auditorium with the wide stage and fairly elaborate backscene of the very earliest Roman theatres. The auditorium of a Greek theatre, set against the slope of a hill, usually curved for rather more than a semi-circle round a circular dancing area (*orchestra*) where the chorus of the play performed its dances; quite separate from this auditorium, and divided from it by open passage-ways known as *parodoi*, stood the stage, which was fairly narrow (little wider than the diameter of the *orchestra*), and which was backed by a scene-building which became increasingly elaborate as time went on. By contrast, the primitive Roman theatre had no proper auditorium at all—certainly not a raised one—but simply contained an area where the audience stood or, later, sat on benches. In front of this was the stage which—to judge from hints in the texts of our only surviving Roman plays, the Romanised Greek comedies of Plautus and Terence—was quite wide; behind this stage stood a building, the front of which doubled as the stage 'set' of house or palace façades (the customary, though not invariable, setting for the dramas), presumably adapted from or influenced by the more elaborate scene-buildings of the later Greek theatres of the Hellenistic age in south Italy and Sicily. When, with their love of enclosure and their fondness for viewing buildings as interiors, Roman architects united this rather 'un-Greek' stage with the Greek auditorium, the resulting adjustments brought about the most important of the differences between the two types of theatre which have been hinted at earlier.

Uniting the two meant that the sloping, curved auditorium (which the Romans called the *cavea*), and the *orchestra* which it surrounded, were reduced to a strict semi-circle. The resultant reduction in the size of the *orchestra* did not create a great problem, since in much Roman drama (as we can see from Plautus and Terence) the role of the chorus was reduced to practically nothing, and such dancing as there was could easily have been accommodated on the wide Roman stage. So the smaller *orchestra* now became used as an extension of the spectators' area, and a considerable amount of it was taken up by three or four shallow steps round the outside of the semi-circle, on which were placed moveable chairs for important members of the audience; their privileged position was often stressed, as at Palmyra, by a low wall which separated the *orchestra* from the rows of less distinguished spectators seated in the *cavea* itself. The long stage (*pulpitum*) was often as much as twice as wide as the *orchestra*, extending along beside the *cavea* on either side. Behind it, and extending its full length, was the façade of the scene-building, known as the *scaenae frons*; this was connected to the *cavea* at either end by lateral return-walls called *versurae* which thus marked the limits of the stage at either side. Both the *scaenae frons* and the *versurae* were as high as the top of the *cavea*, and occasionally, as at Orange (pl. 23), even higher; the *versurae* were connected to the top outer corners of the *cavea* by walls running at right angles, right up against the ends of the upper rows of seating. In place of the open *parodoi* of the Greek theatre, there were vaulted, tunnel-like passages running beneath the seating of the *cavea* on each side and opening into the *orchestra* (pl. 22); these gave access to the seats in the *orchestra*, and to the lower rows of the *cavea*. The upper rows of seats in the *cavea* often extended over these passages, though sometimes this part of the auditorium was occupied by special 'boxes' for distinguished spectators. The theatre-building was thus totally enclosed, and, whereas a Greek audience was able to look out over the scene-building of a Greek theatre into the surrounding countryside, the Roman audience was presented only with the wide, high wall of the *scaenae frons.*

This huge area (at Aspendos it is 62.5m wide and 23m high) was not left blank, but gave full scope for the Romans' love of elaborate decoration. Its great width and most of its considerable height were fronted by two or three superimposed tiers of columns standing clear of the wall, which carried projecting entablatures or triangular, curved or segmental pediments, and flanked niches and *aediculae* containing statues (fig. 38). Often this decoration was carried round the *versurae* as well. The precise style of the ornamentation naturally varied widely, both in its architectural detail and in the nature of the materials used. Two main types, called 'eastern' and 'western' are often distinguished, though, as with Greek and Roman theatres, a distinction by area is hardly possible. The so-called 'eastern' type, typified by Aspendos, is largely regular and rectilinear, while in the 'western' type, of which Orange and Sabratha in Tripolitania (fig. 39) are typical, the columns are set at the front of projections built out from the *scaenae frons* with recessed *exedrae* in between. In both types the whole picture presented a strongly contrasting interplay of bright, sunlit stone and deep shadow. Today, the easily removable elements of this composition have often largely disappeared, though sometimes enough traces remain to enable a partial or, as at Sabratha, almost complete reconstruction from reassembled fragments and modern substitutions—even occasionally where the *scaenae frons* itself has gone.

Such extravagant ornament had evolved as an early element of the design, since it was this part of Scaurus' temporary theatre at Rome which so shocked the elder Pliny. The riot of sculptural detail must have been distracting for the audience, but at least it largely dispensed with the need for scenery. At the level of the lowest tier of columns, three—occasionally, as at Aspendos and Palmyra, five—doors led on to the stage, the central one (*porta regalis*) larger than the flanking ones (*portae hospitales*). These, with the imposing architectural elements beside and above them, were enough to suggest the house or palace façades of the normal setting for drama. Very often, too, there was also a doorway in each of the *versurae* for use by characters entering from the 'wings'.

The stage itself was deep as well as wide; at Orange, for example, its front wall is 13.2m from the *scaenae frons.* Its very depth may have been as crucial as its width in determining the design of the unified Roman theatre-building. It may have influenced the reduction of the *cavea* and *orchestra* to strict semicircular form; but equally it may have been the result of that reduction. The front wall was often an elaborate composition, with carved semicircular and rectangular *exedrae*; the best example is at

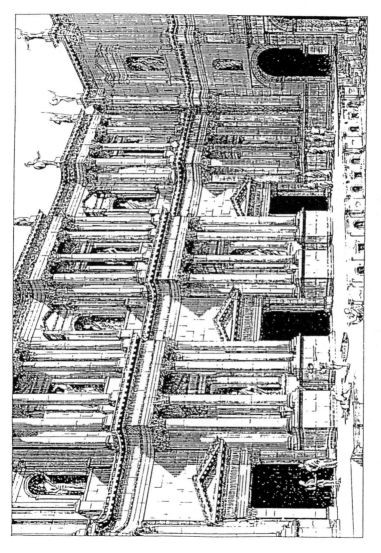

Fig. 38: Gerasa (Jerash), south theatre; reconstruction of *scaenae frons*.

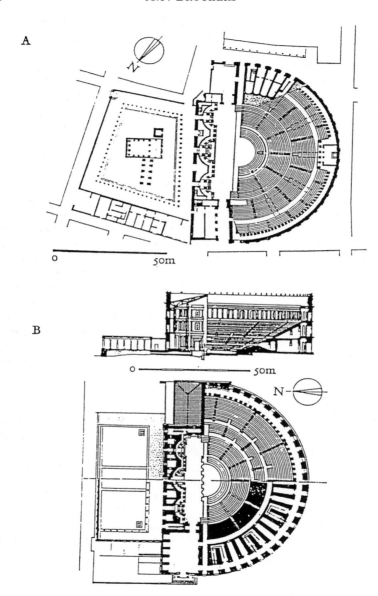

Fig. 39: Plans of theatres in Tripolitania: (A) Lepcis Magna, A.D. 1–2; (B) Sabratha, last quarter of second century A.D.

Sabratha, where these *exedrae* and the straight sections of wall between them are faced with richly carved marble panels. Just behind the front wall ran a deep trough or slot for the curtain (*aulaeum*), which, in direct contrast to those in modern theatres, was lowered into the trough at the start of a performance and raised from it at the end;[7] the curtain was often embroidered with figures which could be thought of as raising the curtain themselves as they rose into view.[8] This trough is still visible in many theatres; at Arles and Orange one can also see the sockets for the posts from which it hung. There were also smaller curtains called *siparia* which could be hung in front of parts of the *scaenae frons* and drawn up or aside when not needed.[9]

Above the stage was a wooden roof, sloping backwards and downwards towards the *scaenae frons*. This is clear at Aspendos and Orange from traces on the upper parts of the *versurae* and from sockets for its beams along the top of the *scaenae frons* itself. The function of this roof may have been partly to protect the performers from the weather, but more importantly it acted as a sounding-board to deflect the words and music towards the audience instead of their being lost in the open air.

The *scaenae frons* was usually the front wall of a rectangular building, the *scaena*, the interior of which was presumably used for green rooms, changing rooms and storage. This is the position at Aspendos, but at Orange and Sabratha the *scaenae frons* is simply a wall, not the front of a building. Here, the extra accommodation needed to mount productions was obtained in two large rooms created by extending the *scaenae frons* at either side until it met walls extending at right angles to it from the outer corners of the *cavea*; there were also small, isolated rooms formed behind the forward projections from the *scaenae frons* on to the stage. In both types the back of the theatre presented a large, comparatively featureless expanse to the outside world—a typical example of the lack of interest which the Romans often showed in the exteriors of their buildings.

At Orange the rear wall (pl. 24), extending as it does the full width of the *cavea*, is 103m long and 36m high. Two rows of corbels project from its upper part, the higher row pierced, the lower row merely with circular depressions in their upper surface; a rounded band of masonry runs along between the two rows, but this, like the cornice which tops the wall, is pierced to allow the erection of masts in the corbels only for a limited section towards each end. This proves that masts could only have been used to hold the ropes of the awning (*velum* or *velarium*) which commonly covered the *cavea* to protect spectators from sun and rain; there could have been no masts in the central section of the wall to hold chains or ropes supporting the stage roof, as has sometimes been suggested. A similar double row of corbels runs along the back of the theatre at Aspendos; in both buildings, one must postulate the existence of similar corbels round the semicircular exterior of the *cavea*.

An innovation in Roman theatres was the frequent provision, as an integral element in the design,[10] of shelter for members of the audience before, between and after performances. This took the form of covered porticoes, of which there were two types—a semicircular one, called the *porticus in summa cavea*, curving round the *cavea* above and behind the topmost row of seating (for example at Aspendos, Bosra, and Vasio [Vaison-la-Romaine] in Provence), and a square or rectangular one, the *porticus post scaenam*, at ground level behind the rear wall of the *scaena* (as at Ostia and the large theatre at Pompeii); occasionally, as at Sabratha, Lepcis Magna (fig. 39) and Amman, a theatre had both. Incidentally, the fact that the *porticus post scaenam* of the large theatre at Pompeii was converted into a gladiatorial barracks in the reign of Nero is eloquent testimony to the decline of the entertainments of the theatre under the early empire and the corresponding rise in popularity of the amphitheatre. At Amman and Lepcis, and at Vienna (Vienne) in France, there was a small temple or shrine in the centre of the *porticus in summa cavea*, while at Lepcis and Ostia there was a temple in the middle of the *porticus post scaenam*; this shows that the early association of theatres with religious centres was not always totally abandoned, though the connection was by no means always kept up.

One of the most significant features of Roman theatre construction has not yet been mentioned because, though common, it is not an essential element of the design—namely that the Romans often built their theatres as completely free-standing buildings. It is not that they always did so, but rather that they did not always have to rely on the presence of a suitably sloping hillside against which to place the auditorium, as the Greeks had normally done. Thus there is great variation between theatres in this respect; at Amman, Aspendos, Orange, Vaison and Vienne, for example, they were built up against steep hillsides, but at Rome both Pompey's theatre and the earliest one in the capital of which anything significant survives, the theatre of Marcellus dedicated in 13 B.C. (fig. 40), were built completely free-standing, as were those of Arles, Bosra, Ostia, Palmyra and Sabratha.

Effectively, then, the Romans, unlike the Greeks, could build their theatres wherever they liked, though a free-standing theatre would obviously be more complicated and expensive to erect than one set against a hill. But the Romans certainly had the necessary skills to do this if they wished; their ability to use the arch and the vault (which we have already noticed in the replacement of the open *parodoi* of the Greeks by tunnels leading

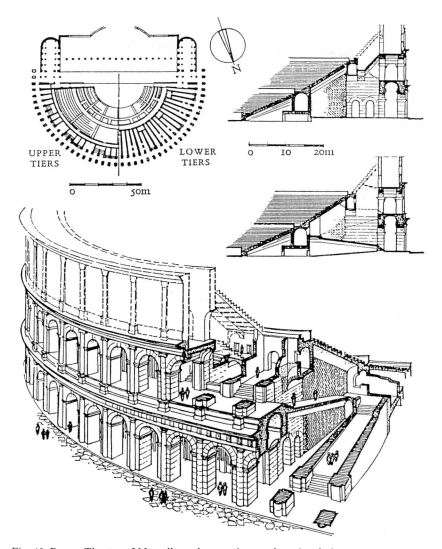

UPPER
TIERS

LOWER
TIERS

0   10   20m

0   50m

Fig. 40: Rome, Theatre of Marcellus: plan, sections and sectional view.

under the *cavea* into the *orchestra*), and their ability to work in concrete, meant that—again in contrast to the Greeks—they were well able to construct the massive substructures on which a free-standing *cavea* would have to be raised. Moreover, the free-standing theatre had a great advantage, in that access to the seating area could be vastly improved by a system of radiating and concentric passages, corridors, walls and stairways placed under the *cavea* itself, with exits (*vomitoria*) giving on to it at various points. The vast numbers of people which the larger theatres could accommodate— examples holding over 6,000 are not uncommon—were thus enabled to enter and leave without undue delay, queuing or crush, proceeding directly to the *vomitorium* nearest to their seats.

We know that at least some of the seating was numbered; in the south theatre at Gerasa (Jerash), for example, the numbers can still be seen carved into the stone. In all theatres, the *cavea* was divided vertically by stairways into wedge-shaped sections called *cunei*, and horizontally by curving cross-aisles (*praecinctiones*) running right round the semi-circle. In theatres built against hills, spectators had to proceed to their seats by moving up from the *orchestra* or down from the top of the *cavea*, and round the *praecinctiones*. In free-standing theatres, however, they could climb up through the substructure of the *cavea* to the *vomitorium* on the appropriate *praecinctio* which was nearest the appropriate *cuneus*.

Few of the surviving free-standing theatres have much of the curving exterior wall of the *cavea* remaining. It has disappeared at Arles and Palmyra and is completely hidden by an Arab fortress at Bosra; but quite an amount does remain at Sabratha, and the best example is the theatre of Marcellus at Rome, which was converted into a fortress and later into a palace. As part of the palace's curving outer wall, two tiers of twelve arches (from a probable forty-one) survive from the theatre; the arcades are framed within engaged columns carrying entablatures, Doric on the first storey and Ionic on the second. Remains of the substructures of the *cavea* beneath the palace show that there must have been a third level, though it is uncertain whether this was a Corinthian arcade or an attic storey. The general lines of the exterior wall of such free-standing theatres, and the arrangement of stairs, passages and corridors under the *cavea*, are best inferred from better-preserved surviving amphitheatres.

It is known that some Roman theatres, as well as providing the setting for plays and mimes, were also used for very different types of entertainment, principally aquatic displays and gladiatorial and animal fights; changes had therefore to be made to accommodate such shows. The theatre at Ostia, for example, built under Augustus and rebuilt and enlarged under Commodus and Septimius Severus, was adapted towards the end of the fourth century A.D. to enable the staging of 'water-ballets'. To this end, the *orchestra* was altered so that it could be flooded, and cisterns to hold the large amount of water needed were inserted into two large rooms (formerly shops) on either side of the entrance to the theatre from the *decumanus maximus* of the town. As for the staging of gladiatorial contests and animal baiting—spectacles more commonly associated with the amphitheatre— this happened particularly in the Greek areas of the empire, where amphitheatres themselves were rare.[11] The best examples (among many such 'hunting theatres')[12] are at Corinth, where both the large theatre and the small theatre (*odeum*) were altered in this way. Their stages and their first few rows of seats were removed to provide room for fights, the enlarged central area was entirely surrounded by a wall built for the spectators' protection, and extra space was provided for animal dens. The case of the large theatre is particularly instructive: having been converted into a 'hunting theatre' early in the third century A.D., it was converted back into a theatre again later in the same century after Corinth had been provided with an amphitheatre (the only one known on the Greek mainland); but this time provision for aquatic displays was incorporated in the updated design. More straightforwardly, some theatres, such as that at Stobi in Jugoslav Macedonia, were deliberately built to double as amphitheatres from the outset, doubtless from motives of economy; such 'theatre-amphitheatres' are found particularly at the northern extremities of the empire, including Britain, where the theatre at Verulamium is of this type.

In many cases, the timing of these changes is significant, and these alternative uses for theatres are eloquent testimony to the decline in cultural and intellectual standards in the later empire; it is small wonder that Christian apologists such as Tertullian[13] were almost as scathing about the entertainments of the theatre as they were about those of the amphitheatre. And it is not only Roman theatres that were subject to this debasing treatment; even the most sacred of Greek theatres, that of Dionysus at Athens, was adapted during the Roman empire for gladiatorial contests[14] and, later, too, for aquatic performances.

Finally, something must be said about *odea*. The *odeum*, the name of which derives from the famous *odeion* built by Pericles in Athens in the fifth century B.C., was a music hall or recital room for lectures, readings, declamations, musical contests or concerts. It catered for more refined tastes than the theatre, and it is significant that *odea* occur less frequently than theatres and are mostly found in those parts of the empire where Greek influence was strong; it is probably even more significant that only one is known in Rome itself, that built by Domitian.[15] Smaller than theatres and usually holding perhaps 1,000 or 1,500 people, *odea* are of two types—open ones, as at Corinth, which are simply smaller versions of full-sized theatres, and covered ones, where the curved seating is enclosed within a square building which once carried a roof. The best example of the latter type, known as a *theatrum tectum* (roofed theatre), is the so-called small theatre at Pompeii mentioned earlier (p. 102), built shortly after 80 B.C. Here the sides of the *cavea* are cut off to enable the theatre to fit into the square, and staircases fill the spaces between the curve of the *cavea* and the back corners. These buildings had to be limited in size if the audience's vision was not to be interfered with by supports holding up the roof, as had been the case with Pericles' *odeion*; but as the entertainments provided in them probably had only a limited appeal, this may well never have been a great problem.

The covered versions owe much to such buildings as the second-century B.C. *bouleuterion* or council chamber at Miletos, and some so-called *odea* may have in fact been *bouleuteria* of this sort, or have served a double purpose as council chambers and concert halls. But the fact that, as at Pompeii, one of these buildings is often found in close proximity to a full-sized theatre—Amman, Corinth and Lyon, and Sillyon and Termessos in southern Turkey, are other examples—shows that many were definitely concert halls situated in an 'entertainment complex'.

II. Amphitheatres

The most notorious of the Romans' entertainments are those of the amphitheatre. To many people the greatest (to some the only) faults in the Roman character are their great cruelty, their seemingly insatiable lust for blood and their total lack of regard for the sanctity of human (let alone animal) life; and these characteristics are most clearly seen in the bloody spectacles presented regularly to tens of thousands of spectators in the many amphitheatres of the Roman world. Such entertainments began in a small way, but quickly grew in size and elaboration as the jaded appetites of easily bored spectators demanded ever bigger, better and more novel shows. The history of gladiatorial contests will serve as a good example to illustrate the general trend: the Romans believed that they had borrowed the idea of gladiators from the Etruscans, and the first such show at Rome was put on by the sons of D. Brutus Pera in the Cattle Market (Forum Boarium) at their father's funeral games in 264 B.C.;[16] in 216 B.C. twenty-two pairs of gladiators appeared at the funeral games of M. Aemilius Lepidus in the Forum Romanum;[17] by 65 B.C. Caesar, as aedile, was exhibiting 320 pairs at his games,[18] and later Augustus was to boast of producing 10,000 gladiators at eight sets of games;[19] but even this vast number must have appeared small by A.D. 107, when Trajan exhibited 10,000 on a single occasion at the games to celebrate the end of the Dacian Wars. The slaughter of wild animals was similarly prodigious; it is Augustus again who says[20] that on the twenty-six occasions when he gave shows involving wild beasts from Africa, a total of 3,500 were killed. As for the later empire, our sources contain many accounts of the exquisite cruelties and awful carnage at such shows; even allowing for exaggeration, the general picture is clear.

The effect of all this slaughter and cruelty on the minds and characters of those who witnessed it is not hard to imagine. St Augustine's account in his *Confessions* of how a respectable law student friend was caught up in the unhealthy atmosphere makes instructive reading.[21] In addition, hooliganism and disorderly behaviour among the excited crowds must have been fairly frequent. Tacitus[22] describes a riot between the people of Pompeii and those of neighbouring Nuceria at gladiatorial games in Pompeii's amphitheatre in A.D.59, as a result of which several Nucerians were killed and many wounded; the punishment was severe: the Roman senate closed the amphitheatre for ten years—the equivalent of closing a football stadium for a similar period today. A vigorous wall-painting, found in Pompeii in 1869 and now in the Naples Museum, preserves a record of the event.

While these types of spectacle remained simple and modest, there was no need for a special building to house them. Vitruvius, though he spends much time discussing theatres, hardly mentions amphitheatres, but instead stresses the need to bear in mind the staging of shows when designing *fora*.[23] We have seen that the shows of 264 and 216 B.C. were indeed held in *fora*, and when Augustus speaks of the killing of the 3,500 African animals, he mentions the circus and forum before the amphitheatre. Clearly, in the early days any large space with reasonable accommodation for spectators, such as the Forum Romanum, Forum Boarium or Circus Maximus, would do; but equally it is clear that by Augustus' day the amphitheatre had been devised as a purpose-built structure for at least the more elaborate spectacles. The evolution of the modern cricket ground or football stadium provides a close parallel.

Unlike the theatre, the amphitheatre is a Roman building with no direct Greek ancestors. The great majority of known examples are in the western half of the empire—in Italy itself, Illyricum, North Africa, Germany, Spain, Gaul and Britain. By contrast, there are few in the eastern half, where Greek influence was strong. Some possible reasons for this, and for the use in those areas of theatres to stage similar spectacles, have already been explained,[24] and, if they are correct, there is perhaps no better testimony to the greater humanity of the Greek spirit. Corinth has the only amphitheatre so far identified on the Greek mainland, and is thus the exception that proves the rule, for that city, refounded by Julius Caesar in 44 B.C. just over a century after its destruction by L. Mummius Achaicus, was essentially Roman, not Greek. There is, significantly, an amphitheatre in Gortyn, which was the Roman administrative centre on Crete, and there are a number scattered through Asia Minor and further east in Judaea.

The word 'amphitheatre' is derived from a Greek adjective meaning 'having seats for spectators all round', and one of its first occurrences as a noun in Latin is in the statement by Augustus just mentioned, at which time the building was obviously still something of a novelty. The first permanent amphitheatre in Rome was that of T. Statilius Taurus dedicated in 30 or 29 B.C.,[25] and the earliest one of any type there to which reference is made dates from little more than twenty years before that. This was an extraordinary building put up by C. Scribonius Curio in 52 B.C.; according to the Elder Pliny,[26] it was built as two theatres back to back, which could be rotated on pivots through 180 degrees to form an amphitheatre, though it is difficult to see how this could have worked in practice. Pliny goes on to comment that Curio devised this novelty because he could not hope to outdo in magnificence the theatre put up by Scaurus six years earlier (see above, p. 101), and adds that the strange contraption was as dangerous for the spectators as it was for the gladiators.

But the earliest amphitheatre of which there is any evidence at all is not in Rome, but at Pompeii, and it still exists in a remarkably complete state (pl. 25). It dates from around 80 B.C. and was erected for the inhabitants of the Sullan colony by the same two local magistrates as built the (similarly significant) *odeum* there. Its early date is evidence for a long and strong tradition of gladiatorial combat in Campania, and, though it lacks the sophistication and technical skill of later examples like those at Capua (S. Maria Capua Vetere) and Puteoli (Pozzuoli) in Campania and the great Flavian amphitheatre (commonly called the Colosseum) at Rome, it has great importance in the history of architecture as the first in a long line of buildings which reaches down to the Olympic stadia of today.

Like all amphitheatres, it consists of rows of raised seating entirely surrounding a flat area, the *arena* (so called from the Latin word for 'sand' with which it was covered), in which the shows took place; and like most amphitheatres it is elliptical or oval in plan, in this case 135m long by 105m wide. It stands on a roughly north–south axis and held some 20,000 people. From outside, it does not appear particularly tall, because the arena and most of the lowest of the three tiers (*maeniana*) into which the inside seating is divided are below surrounding ground level. The excavated earth helped to form the great oval bank on which the seats—at first wooden, but later replaced in stone—were laid. This bank is supported on its outside by a broad wall of concrete faced with *opus incertum* (cf. p. 37), which is in its turn strengthened by buttresses joined by arches to form blind arcading. Since the earth bank is solid, Pompeii's amphitheatre lacks the great number of entrances all round and the internal access corridors and staircases at various levels which typify many later examples. There are, in fact, only three major and two smaller tunnels through the bank: one at the north and one at the south lead to the two main entrances into the arena, used by the combatants, at either narrow end—though since the building is built close up against the south-east corner of the town walls, the tunnel from the south entrance takes a sharp bend to the west and comes out near the south end of the west side; another tunnel leads into the arena from the middle of the west side, and was either the entrance for the magistrates and other notables who occupied the lowest tier of seats, or was the *porta Libitinensis*, the gate of Libitina, goddess of corpses, by which the dead were dragged from the arena. The two smaller tunnels also lead from the west side, not into the arena, but into two sections of an oval passage running round behind the lowest tier of seats and under the middle tier; this gives access to the first two tiers, but is in four disconnected sections, the other two of which have no direct access from outside. The distinguished spectators who sat in the lowest tier of seats were separated from the arena in front by a protective wall over 2m high which was once topped with a grille or railing, and from the lesser mortals behind by another, lower wall. The topmost tier was probably occupied by women, and a terrace of small 'boxes', probably a later addition, runs round the very top of the building. Access to these upper levels is by external staircases which rise to the top of the third tier, two double ones on the west side and two single ones near the north and south ends. Like most amphitheatres, it was provided with an awning, which is seen in position along its east side in the wall-painting showing the riot.

By the very nature of the building, filling and emptying an amphitheatre was at least twice as large a problem as filling and emptying a theatre, and getting 20,000 people in and out of Pompeii's somewhat primitive example must have taken a very long time. This, and the fact that, while it was comparatively easy to find a hillside against which to place a theatre, it would be much more difficult to find a suitable hollow or depression in which to set an amphitheatre, meant that most amphitheatres were, like Pompeii's, free-standing; but it also meant that many later, larger ones were, unlike Pompeii's, not built up on solid earthen banks, but had their seats raised on elaborate concrete and masonry constructions containing the radiating and concentric ramps, corridors and staircases which have already been mentioned in connection with free-standing theatres.

Such arrangements are well seen at the two Provençal amphitheatres of Arles and Nîmes. These two well-preserved buildings are roughly contem-

porary with one another and of very similar design; but there is a lack of
hard evidence by which to date them, and they have been assigned to most
points in the period from the late first century B.C. to the early second
A.D. The one at Arles is slightly the larger of the two (136m by 107m, as
opposed to 130m by 101m), but it is not quite so complete in that it lacks
its low attic storey and its seating is less well preserved. At Nîmes, however,
(pls. 26 and 27) the low attic is intact to the extent that most of the 120
holes for the awning masts around its exterior are still there, and the seats
still rise in places to the very top. Outside below the attic there are, as at
Arles, two superimposed arcades of sixty arches, the lower framed within
engaged Doric pilasters, the upper within engaged Doric columns, each
set bearing an entablature. Inside at ground level two concentric barrel-
vaulted corridors run all round the building under the seating; the outer
one is connected by sloping passages to the slightly lower inner one, from
which staircases lead at regular intervals to *vomitoria* among the lowest of
the four tiers of seats. At second-storey level a corridor roofed with flat
lintels runs round directly above the outer of the two lower ones, and this
is the starting point for three sets of staircases: the first set leads down
to a barrel-vaulted mezzanine corridor (also accessible by stairs leading up
from the outer of the two lower corridors), which gives access by stairs and
vomitoria to the second tier; the second set leads directly to *vomitoria* on
the third tier; and the third set leads off the second and on up to a smaller
gallery running round the building at attic level whence staircases lead to
the *vomitoria* of the fourth, topmost tier. Finally, there are tiny service
stairways rising from the attic-level gallery to the very top of the building
for those who worked the awning.

Another refinement lacking at Pompeii is the elaborate system of pas-
sageways, dens for beasts and criminals, and spaces for machinery to lift
scenery and cages, which in more advanced amphitheatres filled the area
underneath the arena itself. In the Flavian amphitheatre (Colosseum) in
Rome all these close-packed chambers are clearly seen, albeit in a damaged
state, because the arena floor above them has disappeared. Better preserved
are those beneath the amphitheatres of Capua and Pozzuoli in Campania,
where the arena floor is still in place and the subterranean structures are
therefore in good condition, even though the upper parts of both buildings
are ruinous. Pozzuoli provides perhaps the best example. This large amphitheatre (149m by 116m) was built by Vespasian to replace a smaller one
of Augustan date and held between 35,000 and 40,000 spectators; but the
substructures are probably later, of the time of Trajan or Hadrian. Round
the edge of the arena floor runs a ring of some forty square openings, once
containing trap doors, for hauling up cages, with a further sixteen nearer

the middle, and a long, wide opening for raising scenery running down the centre. The actual underground area was reached by sloping ramps running down from arena level at each end of the long axis, and, after the caged animals and scenery had been taken down, these would have been closed off by heavy wooden doors. Underneath (pl. 28), an elliptical barrel-vaulted corridor runs round under the outside of the arena, its roof pierced by the forty square openings already mentioned. Built into the upper outer sides of this corridor is a series of small chambers for the cages, one in line with each of the square openings in the roof of the corridor. In front of each chamber, corbels project from the corridor walls; these would have supported wooden planking on to which a cage was dragged when required, before being hoisted up through the corridor roof into the arena. All the trap doors, and the covering for the long central opening, would, of course, have been firmly closed during performances. These elaborate and well-planned arrangements are excellent proof of the careful thought and great expense which were lavished on the smooth running of the spectacles.

The high point of elaboration and sophistication in this type of building was reached in the largest amphitheatre of all, the so-called Colosseum in Rome (fig. 41). It is properly termed the 'Flavian amphitheatre', because it was begun by Vespasian, was dedicated in A.D. 80 after his death by his son Titus, and was completed by Titus' brother and successor Domitian. To say that it is huge is almost an understatement: it is approximately 188m long by 156m wide, the arena alone is 86m by 54m (larger than the entire amphitheatres at Caerleon and Chester), and it is over 48m high; estimates of its capacity have varied between 45,000 and 55,000. The enormous weight of the structure is carried by a huge elliptical ring of concrete 52m wide and 12m deep, topped with blocks of travertine; on this stand the travertine piers which are the main weight-bearing elements. The passages, corridors and staircases beneath the sloping *cavea* are arranged on the same principle as those at Nîmes, but the system is necessarily much more intricate and complex; they can readily be seen from outside, since by no means all of the outer wall (nor, indeed, of the first row of supporting piers inside) has survived. But it is the outer wall which is the outstanding feature: most amphitheatres impress only by their size, but here the external appearance is also an aesthetically pleasing one. The wall is of travertine and has four storeys. The first three once had eighty arches flanked by engaged columns carrying continuous entablatures which ran all round the building, the bottom storey being of the Doric order, the second Ionic and the third Corinthian. The fourth, attic, storey consists of a plain wall, once separated into eighty corresponding bays by shallow engaged Corinthian pilasters which carry a large cornice at the very top. There is a

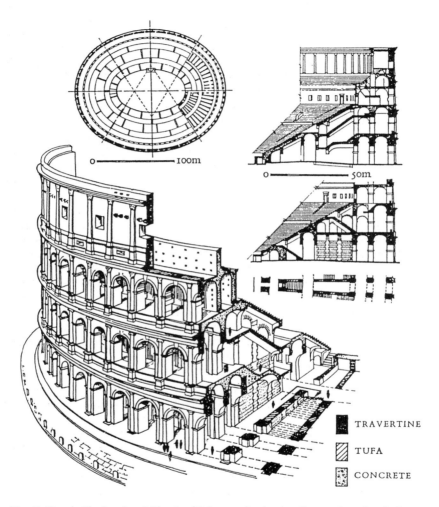

TRAVERTINE

TUFA

CONCRETE

Fig. 41: Rome, Flavian Amphitheatre (Colosseum): plan, sections and sectional view.

large square window in each alternate bay and in the other bays a smaller window in the podium at the bottom; these, like the arches of the lower storeys, provided light for the corridors inside. Halfway up the attic storey there is a row of corbels, three to each bay (and thus once 240 in all) which supported the awning masts which rose up through corresponding holes in the cornice above. The proportions of this massive construction are good: the third (Corinthian) storey is set in about 60cm from the first and second, which are vertically above one another; the shallower pilasters of the attic storey above make that one, too, appear to be further in (though in fact it is not), and the height of the attic is seemingly reduced by being divided into two by the row of corbels. The overall effect is to make the building appear to taper inwards slightly in a way that is most satisfying to the eye.

Of course, by no means all amphitheatres were as sophisticated as those of Rome, Pozzuoli or Nîmes. There were examples to match them elsewhere; at Thysdrus (El Djem) in Tunisia, for instance, the magnificent amphitheatre, which was possibly built to commemorate the proclamation there in A.D. 238 of Gordian I as emperor, clearly shows the influence of the 'Colosseum' on its design. But on the northern fringes of the empire in particular, amphitheatres tended to approximate more to the one at Pompeii than to the 'Colosseum'. The example at Trier on the Moselle in Germany, for instance, has earth banks revetted with stone, and was built around A.D. 100 to replace one of earth and wood; like the more advanced one at Pula in Istria, it is built partly into a hillside, and the earth excavated from that side (and from a cellar under the arena) was used to build up the bank on the other. The one at Lutetia (Paris) is also of earth with retaining walls of stone—though here a stage building at some time replaced the seating along one of the long sides so that it could double as a theatre. And all the amphitheatres in Britain, as at Caerleon, Chester, Cirencester and Silchester, were also of stone- or wood-faced earth banks which were pierced by only a few tunnel-like passages into the arena.

It seems that some amphitheatres had arenas which could be flooded and used for naval battles (*naumachiae*)—though it is difficult to see how those which had many trap doors and openings for scenery could have been made completely watertight. More often, it would appear, such water-borne fights were staged in artificial lakes (also called *naumachiae*) created for the occasion, with, presumably, raised seating provided for the spectators. Augustus[27] talks of one such show he gave across the Tiber in Rome 'at the spot where the grove of the Caesars is now'—words which prove that the place was only temporarily used for that purpose. He gives the dimensions of the site as 1,800 Roman feet long and 1,200 wide (532m by 355m), and adds that thirty beaked ships, triremes and biremes, took part as well as a larger number of smaller vessels, with about 3,000 combatants on board, exclusive of rowers. The fact that such a massive work was undertaken for a single occasion, and that so many men were, quite literally, 'butchered to make a Roman holiday', provides further proof—if proof is needed—of the vast scale attained by such spectacles, and of the vast depths of inhumanity which their organisers—and the spectators—could plumb.

III. Circuses

The third major class of building for entertainment in Rome after the theatre and amphitheatre was the circus. This was, as we have seen (p. 113), used in early days for spectacles later associated with amphitheatres, as it was for several other entertainments, especially athletic events; but right from the start it was primarily associated, and always remained associated, with the sport of chariot racing, for which the Romans developed an enthusiasm which bordered on mania. The circus was thus by quite some time the earliest of Roman buildings for entertainment; and, by the nature of the principal activity held in it, it was also the largest.

The racing was for one-horse chariots or for teams of two, three or four horses. Whatever its organisation in Rome under the Republic—and we know remarkably little about this—by the time of the Empire it had become a highly professional affair, with large stables supplying the horses, chariots and drivers. These stables were named after the colours which the drivers wore—at first only reds and whites, but by the first century A.D. also blues and greens. Domitian's addition of two more, golds and purples, was short-lived, but the first four continued well into the second century, after which the blues took over the reds and the greens the whites, the ousted colours being worn by the second-string riders of the two remaining major stables. The younger Pliny, in a famous letter[28] which tells us as much about the snobbishness of the writer as it does about the races, criticises the spectators' blind devotion to their favoured colour regardless of the horses' speed or their drivers' expertise, and gives a clear, if biased, picture of their passion for the sport. Ovid[29] gives a charming description of a young man out with his girlfriend for a day at the races, and there are numerous other references throughout Latin literature, since the sport, unlike the entertainments of the theatre and—particularly—the amphitheatre, was not suppressed at the triumph of Christianity, but flourished and continued into the Byzantine era. Several of these references attest the popularity of betting on the races,[30] though there does not seem to have been a well-organised betting 'industry' as there is with horse racing or greyhound racing today; instead, a person appears to have placed his bet (*pignus* or *sponsio*) with a friend or fellow-enthusiast on an individual basis. All this literary material is supplemented by a number of inscriptions which record the achievements of charioteers.

Unfortunately, in contrast to the wealth of literary and epigraphical evidence for the sport, the archaeological record for its buildings is not

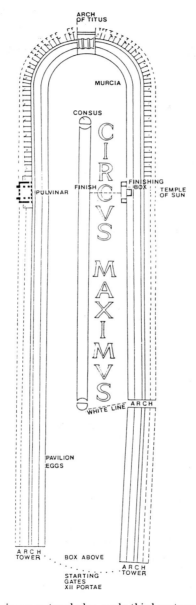

Fig. 42: Rome, Circus Maximus; restored plan, early third century A.D.

strong, and this is perhaps why, until recently, little has been written about them. Few of the many circuses, which are scattered throughout the Roman world (particularly in the West), have been completely excavated. Very little is left of the earliest, largest and most famous of them, the Circus Maximus in Rome (fig. 42), which, among its many vicissitudes, was once the site of Rome's gas works; and others in the capital, such as the Circus of Gaius and Nero or Vatican Circus, the traditional site of St Peter's martyrdom, are even less visible today. But one just outside the city has been completely cleared—the Circus of Maxentius beside the Appian Way (pl. 29); it is a late building of the fourth century A.D., but at least for that reason is an example of a fully-developed design. And in the provinces, the circus at Lepcis Magna which dates from the second century A.D. has also been thoroughly investigated.

The circus has many similarities to the Greek hippodrome, though whether the Romans got the idea of it directly from the Greeks or via the Etruscans is impossible to tell; but Livy's statement[31] that the area for the Circus Maximus was first marked out by King Tarquinius Priscus, who was Etruscan and reigned traditionally from 616 to 579-8 B.C., perhaps lends weight to the latter view. The site chosen was the valley between the Palatine and Aventine hills, whose slopes would have provided room for spectators, and over the centuries it was developed and embellished until by the time of the early empire it formed a huge building some 620m long by 140m wide. Like all circuses it was a long inverted 'U' with the start at the open end; and except at that open end it was, in its developed form, entirely surrounded by raised seating similar to that in free-standing theatres which held, according to the elder Pliny,[32] 250,000 spectators. In the centre of the track towards each end stood the two turning-posts (*metae*), round which the chariots had to pass, and, to eliminate head-on crashes, these were joined by a long, low wall—in simpler circuses probably just an earth bank.[33] In larger circuses this central barrier was ornamented with statues, obelisks etc., and often these have survived where the circus itself has largely gone; two obelisks from the Circus Maximus now stand in the Piazza del Popolo and Piazza di S. Giovanni in Laterano, one from the Vatican Circus is in St Peter's Square, one from the Circus of Maxentius is in the Piazza Navona, and one from the circus at Arles now stands in the Place de la République in that city. Also on the barrier were the lap counters. In the Circus Maximus these were seven discs known as 'eggs', first introduced, according to Livy,[34] in 174 B.C., one of which was lowered as each lap was completed; later there were also seven dolphins, one of which, at the end of each lap, plunged into a water channel which ran along the top of the barrier.

What I have called the 'open' end of the circus was not in fact open, since here stood the starting gates (*carceres*), often with an ornamental arch in their centre for processions to pass through; Livy[35] tells us that in the Circus Maximus these first appeared as early as 329 B.C. To make things fairer for the competitors, the gates were arranged in a shallow arc, but, again for fairness (and also to avoid too many crashes at the very start), the centre of the imaginary circle of which this arc formed a part was somewhere to the right of the near *meta*. Crashes at the start were clearly a great problem, because several other devices were employed, particularly in later circuses, to try to reduce them: a chalk line was marked out across the track, and until they had crossed this the chariots had to keep in lanes; to give more room as chariots approached the near *meta* for the first time, the spectators' seating sometimes bulged outwards at this point; and sometimes, too, for the same reasons the central barrier was skewed slightly to the left at the near end. These last two refinements are visible today in the Circus of Maxentius, and the last one can also be seen in the circus at Lepcis Magna.

The elaborate nature of the buildings used for entertainment in the Roman world and the way in which they were, over the centuries, continually refined and improved are not merely evidence for the great popularity of the sports and spectacles staged in them; they also add point to the fact that the provision of recreation for the masses was, in the eyes of the authorities, an absolute necessity. If it were not kept amused, the vast and largely idle population of Rome and other large cities would become restive and threaten stability. But the authorities, in trying to head off this threat, found themselves caught in a vicious circle; the more public entertainment they provided, the more the people came to expect it as of right. Realisation of this fact will go a long way towards explaining why the Romans were prepared to house these entertainments in some of the largest, most imposing and most sophisticated buildings of the ancient world.

NOTES

1. Juvenal 10.80–1.

2. Plutarch, *Pompey* 42.4.

3. Livy, epitome of book 48.

4. Aulus Gellius 10.1.7.

5. *Natural History* 36.113–115.

6. *Annals* 14.21.

7. Horace, *Epistles* 2.1.189; Cicero, *pro Caelio* 65.

8. Ovid, *Metamorphoses* 3.111-14; Virgil, *Georgics* 3.25.

9. Apuleius, *Metamorphoses* 10.29.

10. Vitruvius 5.9.1.

11. It is often assumed that the reason for the absence of amphitheatres in the Greek world lies in the fact that the type of show put on in them did not appeal to the more cultured Greek mind, and that provision of such entertainments within the smaller compass of adapted theatres therefore sufficed to satisfy the needs of the less cultured expatriate Romans and Roman garrisons in the vicinity. Hard evidence for this view is lacking, though the assumption may not be without some foundation.

12. Dio Cassius 78.9.7.

13. *De spectaculis* 10.1; 17.1.

14. Dio Chrysostom, *Oration* 31.121.

15. Suetonius, *Domitian* 5.

16. Valerius Maximus 2.4.7; Livy, epitome of book 16.

17. Livy 22.30.15.

18. Plutarch, *Caesar* 5.4.

19. *Res Gestae* 22.1.

20. *Res Gestae* 22.3.

21. 6.8. For instance, he tells us that when the young man, who had kept his eyes tight shut as he sat in his place, at last opened them, '... he instantly drank in the savagery; he did not turn his head away, but kept his gaze fixed, unknowingly imbibing the madness and revelling in the wickedness of the fight, intoxicated with bloodthirsty joy. He was not now the man who had come, but was one of the crowd he had joined, and a true companion of those who had brought him along.'

22. *Annals* 14.17.

23. 5.1.1-2.

24. See note 11 above.

25. Suetonius, *Augustus* 29.5.

26. *Natural History* 36.116-20.

27. *Res Gestae* 23.

28. 9.6.

29. *Amores* 3.2; cf. *Art of Love* 1.135ff.

30. Juvenal 11.201-2; Martial 11.1.15-16; Petronius 70.13.

31. 1.35.8.

32. *Natural History* 36.102.

33. Apparently ancient writers—unlike many modern authorities—did not call this central barrier a *spina*. Some later ones, however, did refer to it as a *euripus* ('strait'

or 'channel'), doubtless because of the water channel or water-filled basins which in later times were sometimes situated on it (see below).

34. 41.27.6.

35. 8.20.1.

5. Aqueducts

A. TREVOR HODGE

*Tot aquarum tam multis necessariis molibus pyramidas vide-
licet otiosas compares aut cetera inertia sed fama celebrata
opera Graecorum.*

I ask you! Just compare this vast array of indispensable structures carrying so much water with the idle Pyramids or the
world-famous but useless monuments of the Greeks.[1]

Sextus Julius Frontinus' appointment by the Emperor Nerva in 97 A.D.
as Director of the Rome Metropolitan Waterworks (*curator aquarum*) was
something of an experiment. The Roman imperial administration was then
grappling with a question not unknown in modern business: is management
a universally applicable art, so that a man trained in it can efficiently run
any large enterprise, no matter what line of business it is actually engaged
in; or is it better, even essential, to have the detailed, inside knowledge of the
actual product that can come only from having spent one's life in the trade?
Frontinus, a distinguished ex-army officer with no experience in hydraulic
engineering, was appointed largely as an exercise of the new imperial policy
of appointing managers to manage, and his vigorous administration, as his
new broom swept through the cobwebs of a corrupt Department, was no
doubt largely to be seen as a public justification of his Emperor's policy.
Faced with a highly technical field that any engineer would tell him needed
a lifetime to master (and no doubt there were many in Rome who did), the
test case worked. And it was no doubt to demonstrate that it really had

worked, that he really had mastered the intricate technicalities of Rome's water supply and was not merely acting as a front man or rubber-stamp for his subordinates, that Frontinus published his book *The Aqueducts of Rome*. Today, this work provides a good half of our information on the Roman aqueducts; the other half is provided by archaeological study of the actual remains.

But there is another reason why this chapter should begin with Frontinus. He was not only proud of the technical details of the subject he had learned, he was also convinced that water supply was a great and important responsibility, and that the calling of Water Commissioner was a noble one. He does not stand alone. His ringing declaration of faith in his office, printed at the head of this chapter, is one to which most Romans would devoutly subscribe, and which has since been echoed by many modern historians. The increasing emphasis on social, as opposed to political, history has led to a widespread reappraisal of the importance of some of the unglamorous necessities of daily life, and it could be, indeed has been, argued that the abundant provision of pure water and hygienic sanitation must rank as one of the greatest achievements of the Roman genius. If one sees Roman aqueducts as essentially on the same level as Roman law, then plainly they must be included in any book dealing with Roman affairs.

But there is another side to the question. One man's necessity is another man's luxury, and one can easily argue that the aqueducts were an idle superfluity, an expensive waste of time. For one thing, aqueducts were usually built to supply baths, not drinking water, though (once in place) they were used for that too. Most Roman towns only acquired an aqueduct well on in their history, and before it arrived relied quite happily on wells. London, for example, never had an aqueduct at all. The 'pure water' argument thus largely breaks down. That was not the primary purpose of aqueducts, and pure drinking water could be had independently of them. Moreover, to take an extreme example, the Roman legionaries were accustomed to a high standard of living, with aqueduct-fed baths a regular feature of all permanent camps. When they settled as veterans in north Africa, therefore, they built cities with aqueducts as part of their regular way of life, cities that are today often quoted as evidence of the unparalleled prosperity of the region under Roman rule. But what did the local Berber tribesmen think of them? What was their reaction on seeing their precious water, on which they depended for growing their food in this arid land, channelled away to a town, where the inhabitants wanted it for no better purpose than to splash around in it? One doubts if they shared our enthusiasm for the aqueducts as monuments of progress: considering the legionaries' need of them, they probably also wondered aloud how an empire had ever been carved out by such a manifestly effete race.

There is also another dilemma to affect us if we are considering aqueducts as monuments of Roman glory. In their conventional form, the glory is clear enough. The lofty bulk of the Pont du Gard has spoken to all ages in mute but eloquent tones of grandiloquent magnificence; the ancient traveller, approaching home along the Appian Way and viewing the endless array of aqueduct arcades striding across the Campagna like marching armies, must have felt that here, indeed, was the Eternal City, the very centre of civilisation and the heart of world affairs. Archaeologists and architectural historians have reacted the same way, and countless handbooks on Roman civilisation have carried on their dust covers pictures of the Pont du Gard or other aqueduct arches as the quintessential symbol of its splendours.

We must therefore be very clear that the arches which come automatically to our mind when the word 'aqueduct' is mentioned formed only a very small part of it. Most aqueducts ran on arches for less than 10 per cent of their total length: for the rest, the water channel ran at ground level, or, more often, buried about a metre below it. In its normal form, therefore, the Roman aqueduct was distinctly unspectacular; usually, indeed, it was completely out of sight. The great bridges and viaducts, for all their impressive appearance, were never more than a regrettable necessity upon which the engineers had to fall back when they could not get out of it. Some aqueducts had none at all. The first aqueduct at Rome, the Aqua Appia, was entirely underground. More typical, perhaps, is the 75km long Eifel aqueduct serving Roman Cologne (pl. 30). Its length makes it a major engineering feat, but only rarely does it emerge from below ground and become visible: far from being monumental, even finding and seeing it is impossible without the guidance of knowledgeable local authorities, who know where to go. One must also remember that aqueducts were only one link in the water supply system, and a study limited to them must necessarily omit such features as catchment and urban distribution—in a word, what happened to the water before it got into the aqueduct, and after it left it.

It will thus be seen that a study of Roman aqueducts will be a very different matter depending on one's approach. If one wishes to know how the cities got water, to study the aqueducts as functioning machines rather than static monuments and remains, one will cast one's net much wider. If it is the architectural monuments that are one's concern, one will embark on a study more circumscribed but more detailed, with more emphasis on dating and brick-stamps and less on hydraulics. Both approaches—perhaps we may typify them as the approach of the engineer or social historian, and that of the archaeologist or art historian—are valid, but the student must be clear which one he is dealing with. The warning is necessary because this split does not exist in other forms of Roman architecture, or in other chapters of this book. There are no extensive parts of Roman temples or amphitheatres that are excluded from consideration because they are not monumental, or do not count as architecture. But to study a Roman aqueduct by restricting oneself to the architectural sections of it is like trying to comprehend a complete railway system by looking only at its bridges and viaducts. In a work on Roman monumental architecture that is, of course, exactly what we shall be doing; the reader must therefore be clearly aware of these limitations.

A little technical information is, however, necessary to set these architectural triumphs in context. A Roman aqueduct differed from a modern water supply in five significant ways. First, it operated on the constant offtake principle, and there was usually no water storage to be drawn on as needed. Dams and reservoirs did indeed exist, but were almost all located in Spain (including the three best-known ones, at Cornalvo, Proserpina, and Alcantarilla), north Africa, and the Middle East, where the low rainfall encouraged such conservation measures. Normally, however, the aqueduct was fed by a spring that kept the water coming as fast as it was being used, in much the way that a generating station supplies a modern electric power grid. Second, taps were very little used and all outlets, in principle, were running 24 hours a day. This meant that there were no peak hours, and that accordingly the quantities of water that passed through the system and thus had to be provided (even if not put to actual use) were truly vast, such as to make modern water engineers gasp. Exact figures are out of the question, but estimates for the total volume of water supplied daily to Rome run from half a million to a million cubic metres (see Table, p. 142 below): reduced to a per capita basis, it has been calculated that this gives a water supply in Rome of the first century A.D. almost twice that of New York (the calculated per capita daily water consumption in first-century Rome being 1.4 cubic metres (300 gallons); in New York City (1986) it is 0.87 cubic metres (190 gallons)). Speaking of Roman architecture, Sir Mortimer Wheeler has identified 'the grandest facet of the Roman achievement as a whole: the overall magnitude of its field of thought'.[2] These figures give his words a new weight and relevance.

The third significant fact is that the system operated entirely by gravity flow. Pumps existed and are now known to have been more common than previously thought, but still played no serious part in the aqueducts. The inverted siphon was known and employed, both to cross rural valleys and, in urban distribution, to feed individual outlets in houses from raised tanks

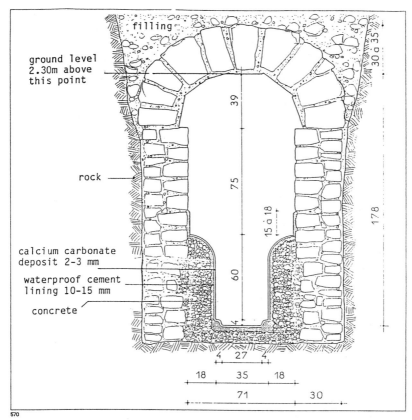

Fig. 43: Cross-section of a typical conduit. Only the narrow, lower section actually carried the water, the upper part being provided to give access to maintenance workers.

at the street corners, but these too operated by gravity. Fourth, the water normally ran in a conduit that, though covered in on top to stop dirt getting into the channel, did not operate like a closed pipe. The conduit was usually only half full, and its dimensions were dictated not by the volume of water carried but by the need for human access for cleaning. Thus all aqueduct channels tend to be around the same size, the actual water being carried sometimes only in a pipeline or gutter in the floor (fig. 43). Normally, it was only when it encountered a siphon that the water, now under pressure because of the dip below natural water level, ran in a pipe and filled it.

Fifth, and lastly, the aqueduct in its channel may well be considered as an artificial river. Depending on rainfall, it had high and low seasons, its varying level playing havoc with modern attempts to estimate volume and flow. Like a river, it could not be shut off (as can a modern pipe, by the turn of a tap), and if you tried, the channel would simply overflow; the water could only be diverted elsewhere.

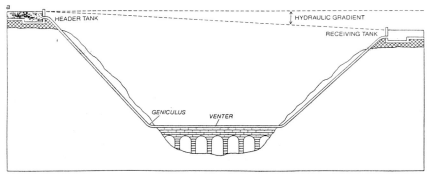

Fig. 44: Diagram illustrating operation of a siphon.

It was the combination of gravity flow and the open channel that led to monumental architecture, in the form of bridges and arcades, and in two quite different ways. First, running under gravity, the water had to arrive at the city still at a good height above ground level if it was ever to serve the higher parts of the town. This meant that if the city was approached across a plain, the aqueduct had to cross it raised on a continuous arcade; it was not a question of bridging some valley in the terrain, but of keeping the water high. This leads to the long arcades of the Roman Campagna (and elsewhere, notably Carthage). Their characteristics are that they are very, very long (some 10km or so, at Rome), and built over flat land. Second, there was distance and gradient. The longest known aqueduct was at Roman Carthage, with a channel length of 132km, but at Rome itself lengths of 80 or 90km were common. If, then, the source was to be far from the city, it also had to be reasonably high, as the entire aqueduct had to run downhill. This meant that the source was often in the mountains, where the engineer was frequently faced with a valley that the channel had to cross. He had three choices. He could contour around it, running up along one side, across the top, and back down the other. In itself this was simple, but if the valley was a long one, it would mean a correspondingly long detour and costs might rise prohibitively high. The governing factor was probably not construction, but maintenance costs. Nearly all Roman aqueducts used hard water that left a caked deposit which would soon choke the channel if it was not regularly cleaned out; the cleaning process was never-ending, and every extra yard of aqueduct was an extra yard to be kept clean. Alternatively, the engineer could cross the valley directly, by an inverted siphon, running the water down one slope in closed pipes (usually of lead and up to nine in number), across the bottom and up the facing slope, where—the water naturally rising back to its own level—the pipes then delivered it back into a conventional aqueduct channel (fig. 44). Often, to reduce the depth to which the pipes plunged and hence the pressure inside them, they were carried over the bottom of the valley on a masonry bridge, the *venter*, which much resembles an ordinary aqueduct arcade and is occasionally mistaken for one. It differs in being much wider, since it carried not only a battery of pipes laid side by side, but also, evidently, a catwalk for maintenance access; its superstructure is also lower, since there is no masonry conduit and the pipes have invariably now disappeared (pl. 31). Despite doubts frequently expressed in modern textbooks, such siphons (it is an established convention among archaeologists so to refer to them, though, strictly speaking, 'inverted siphon' would be the correct term) were relatively common and the Romans had no difficulty making pipes that would withstand the pressure. The largest known is that at Beaunant, near Lyon, which is 2.6 km long, and, with a maximum depth of 123m, is as high as almost three Ponts du Gard one on top of the other. The role of siphons in Roman waterworks has been much underestimated, largely because there were very few in the aqueducts of Rome itself; they are most numerous around Lyon (Lugdunum), which had nine of them, divided among the four aqueducts that served it.

Siphons, however, though technically feasible, were expensive, probably from transport costs of the vast weight of lead needed for the pipes; they must have also been very hard to clean. Usually, therefore, the engineer preferred a bridge, and fell back on the siphon only when a bridge would have been too big to build. The limiting height seems to have been about 50m, the highest aqueduct bridge being the Pont du Gard, in Provence, carrying the aqueduct supplying Nîmes over the river Gardon. It is these bridges in the hill country that form the second category of monumental architecture on aqueducts, and their nature makes them quite different from the arcades crossing the plains. The arcades are very long, relatively low, and over flat ground. The bridges are short, come in a variety of heights, and span valleys. It is common to find both on the same aqueduct.

We will consider bridges first. Leaving aside minor culverts, which were numerous, major bridges usually run to a standard form. The valleys they cross are those of minor streams or of depressions with no water in them at all. There is nothing really to span, and their purpose is rather to maintain the level of the conduit. One thus finds a series of tall, narrow arches, and wide spans are rare. The big central arch (span 24.52m) of the Pont du Gard across the river Gardon is an exception to this, while spans of 22m are found on the Trajanic aqueduct of Antioch and 15.50m in the Ponte San Pietro on the Aqua Marcia at Rome, but all of these are uncommon: most bridges had their piers set at an interaxial interval of about only 7.5m. These repeated arches—in effect a modular system of construction—meant that length was no problem. Height was, and in three ways. First, the higher the piers, the heavier. Whether built of cut stone or of concrete, the piers were strong in compression and could easily carry the extra weight, but when it was transferred to the foundations it was a different story, for if the ground was unstable or the piers ill founded, something might shift under the load. For example, this happened on the Pont de l'Oued Nasara, at Cherchel (Caesarea), in Algeria, where the entire bridge began bodily to slide downhill.

The second problem stemming from height is that if the piers were unduly tall and thin they might tend to buckle and tilt, either along the line of the bridge or crossways to it. One solution to this was to construct the bridge of two or three superimposed tiers of arches, thus effectively limiting the height of each arch and its supporting piers to manageable proportions. The classic example of this is the Pont du Gard (pl. 32), which is, in effect, three self-contained bridges, one on top of the other; it will be noted that none of its piers or arches are particularly tall. The bridges at Segovia (pl. 33) and Tarragona follow the same principle. Another solution was to build a bridge on one single set of tall piers running right through to the top, and then to provide the necessary stability by cross-bracing each one about half way up to its neighbours on either side; the cross-bracing took the form of a brick arch. The best examples of this type are Mérida (fig. 45) (which has braces at two levels, not one), Fréjus, and some of the bridges at Cherchel.

The third problem was lateral stability. Even if the piers were stayed by cross-bracing to each other, the whole bridge, reacting like a wall that had been built too thin, might fall over sideways in its entirety, particularly when subjected to the pressure of strong cross-winds. Two remedies for this were invoked. In a multi-tier aqueduct one could broaden the base by making the tiers progressively thicker towards the bottom. Thus in the Pont du Gard the bottom tier of arches is 6.3m thick, from side to side, the middle one 4.5, and the top one 3.06. Alternatively, the piers could be propped and reinforced by buttresses, as in the very prominent sloping buttresses of the aqueduct at Fréjus (fig. 46). Sometimes the actual piers

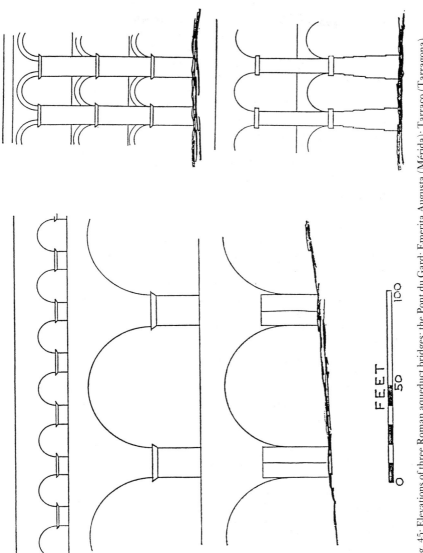

Fig. 45: Elevations of three Roman aqueduct bridges: the Pont du Gard; Emerita Augusta (Mérida); Tarraco (Tarragona).

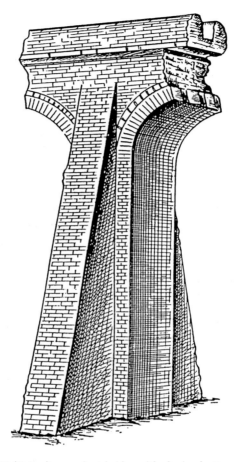

Fig. 46: Forum Iulii (Fréjus): aqueduct bridge with sloping buttresses.

could themselves be tapered to provide a broader base; rather than giving the pier a sloping face, this was normally done by a series of set-backs, the pier itself retaining a vertical face in between (as in the lowest tier at Tarragona (fig. 45) or Metz). It is hard to say how serious a problem this lateral instability presented. The large (288m long by 26m high) Pont de L'Oued Bellah at Cherchel may have owed its eventual collapse to being blown down. On the other hand, striking testimony to the contrary comes from the Pont du Gard, which around the sixteenth century had all its piers on the second tier cut back on one side to permit passage of a carriage road (fig. 47). Of course, the entire structure ought to have tipped over sideways into the river. There could be no more cogent demonstration of the excellence of Roman engineering than the fact that it survived this incredible mutilation for two or three centuries with no apparent ill effects, before eventual reconstruction in 1702 when its original form was restored.

It must be made clear that none of these aqueducts carried roads or even gangways for human passage, though no doubt occasional hardy souls might venture along the top on an 'at your own risk' basis. Of the three bridges carrying roadways today, the Pont du Gard acquired its road access only in 1743-47, the Ponte Lupo (Rome) as a result of rebuilding in antiquity, and Aspendos (Turkey) is highly conjectural and presents serious technical problems in other ways. It was the water channel across the top that counted. The size of this, the *specus*, varied, but dimensions of around 50cm wide by 80 high may be taken as typical. It was lined with waterproof cement which had the added functions of accelerating flow by reducing friction, and, hopefully, retarding the build-up of calcium carbonate deposit. Unlike most road bridges, an aqueduct bridge was not level, but continued the normal downward gradient of the channel, though this is usually too slight to be easily observed by eye; the top of the Pont du Gard, for example, is 11cm lower at one end than the other. Despite generalisations in the handbooks, there was no standardised figure for a Roman aqueduct gradient, and even on individual aqueducts the slope often varies greatly. To give some typical examples, the slope on the Pont du Gard, in metres per kilometre, is 0.4; Ponte San Pietro (Rome), 2.95; Pont de L'Oued Bellah (Cherchel), 5.3; and Pont de L'Oued Ilelouine (Cherchel), 2.6. By comparison the overall average slopes on these aqueducts, from source to city, are 0.34 (Nîmes), 2.7 (Marcia, Rome), and 2.0 (Cherchel). One may risk the generalisation and assert that the gradient usually increased while crossing the bridge.

We must also make special mention of one of the most imposing and unconventional bridges, that at Aspendos, in southern Turkey (pl. 34). This is an 850m long bridge, or arcade, some 16m high, and it carries not a conventional conduit but a stone pipeline in which the water runs under pressure in a siphon. Near each end is an open tank, at natural water level, 29.75m above the normal top of the bridge, supported on a brick and concrete pier that also houses an internal staircase to give access for inspection. The water pipeline climbs up a sloping ramp to the tank, and pours into it; at the other end of the tank the water re-enters a pipe, slopes down again to bridge level, and proceeds on along it to the far end where the whole process is repeated. This results in two great towers, roughly

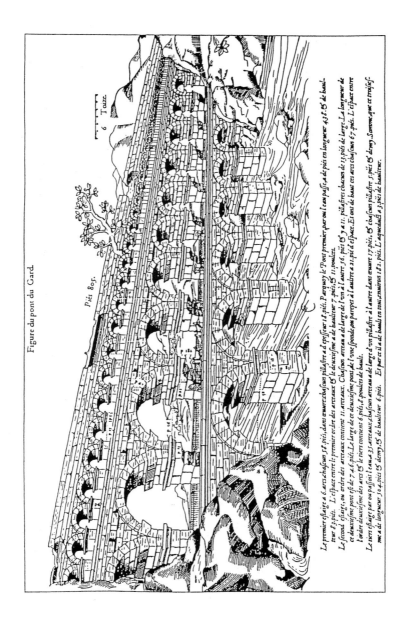

Fig. 47: The Pont du Gard: drawing by Poldo d'Albenas in 1557, showing piers cut back to provide a road crossing.

triangular in profile thanks to the two sloping ramps; the water runs in three consecutive siphons, separated by the two tanks. No convincing explanation of this extraordinary arrangement has yet been found. The English term for the two towers, 'pressure towers',[3] is a misnomer, since they have no effect on pressure, and claims that they reduce friction by allowing trapped air to escape are unfounded.

When one comes to the aesthetics of the bridges, one notes something of a paradox. Many of the bridges were located in remote valleys, off the roadways and natural lines of communication, and can have been admired only by herdsmen and chance wayfarers. Moreover, the frequent repairs and rebuilding to which Roman aqueducts were subject often left them looking like a wreck. The Ponte Lupo is the largest bridge on the Rome aqueducts, and ought to be the queen of the system; in fact it has so suffered from additions, props, and extensions, that it is hard to look at it and see anything but an amorphous and disorganised mess (pl. 35). Even the famous Pont du Gard carries a multiplicity of roughly cut and prominently protruding stones, which originally served as supports for the wooden scaffolding, and were retained to facilitate its re-erection during repairs. And we must always remember the real reason these bridges were built. Technically, they could all have been replaced by siphons, but the lead would have cost more: the bridges are a monument to cheapness.

At this point comes the paradox. As long as they are not disfigured by later accretions, even the simplest of aqueduct bridges are nevertheless aesthetically satisfying. In a way, given the harmonious proportions of Roman piers and arches, it was hard for the engineer not to build a bridge that looked good, but there is more to it than that. To the Romans, the aqueduct system was the focus of a great deal of civic pride, and one has the impression that often, once it was decided in any case to build a large bridge, great attention was then paid to making it attractive and imposing. Certainly, the impressive stature of the Pont du Gard has been sufficiently commanding to induce the French engineers to build in 1847, at Roquefavour, near Aix-en-Provence, a modern and even larger version of it to carry the water supply of Marseille, which was specifically intended both to imitate and outdo it (the Roquefavour bridge is half as large again, and imitates the Pont du Gard so effectively that tourists have been known to take it for a Roman antiquity). Moreover, although at first sight the Pont du Gard seems a work of straightforward and repetitive symmetry, this impression is deceptive. The exigencies of the site called for certain irregularities, and a great deal of care went into the design to conceal them. Thus, the lower arches are not all the same size, the central one being rather larger than the rest. Since the tops of all the arches are on the same level, the bottom of the large one has to come down rather further than its two neighbours, resulting in a pair of piers that are each asymmetrical, being straight on one side and curved on the other. The same thing may be observed on the second tier, which is made to match. On the top tier, the small arches regularly correspond to the spacing of the large ones beneath. Only on closer examination do we notice that while there are three of them over the normal arches, the large central arch has four. It takes an even keener eye to note that the irregularities are accommodated by making some of their piers thicker than others (in pl. 32, compare, on the top tier, the thickness of the first from the left with, e.g. the fourth or fifth). None of this is obvious, and it betokens a very careful and subtle design. We may perhaps infer that while bridges were cheaper than siphons, yet once it had been decided that there was going to be a bridge there anyway, nobody grudged the small extra trouble of making presentable and attractive a structure that was in any case bound to dominate the landscape.

As the aqueduct left the hills and crossed the plain, it was frequently carried on a continuous arcade; as noted, the purpose was to keep the water level high enough to serve the city. This might be accentuated if the city was located, as so many of them were, on an isolated hill or acropolis. This naturally made it harder to bring in an aqueduct, but it must be repeated that most cities were founded without aqueducts, and aqueduct access was not one of the criteria taken into account in their siting. That came later. At Carthage, a section of the aqueduct approached the city across the Miliane plain on an arcade some 4.5km long and 20m high, admired by Arab writers of subsequent centuries as one of the marvels of Africa; but of the various cities so served, at none were the arcades more prominent than at Rome itself. There, the Aqua Marcia alone arrives after crossing the Campagna on a continuous arcade a good 15km long that, by the time it has got to the city, has risen to a height above ground of over 20m. The reader will be surprised at talk of the aqueduct rising—was it not supposed to slope downhill? So it does, but to the observer the conduits, on entering the Campagna, look as if they gradually surface from underground and then slowly climb up into the air, with the arches under them becoming progressively higher. In actual fact, it is the ground that is receding, for though it looks flat the Campagna also slopes downhill, and more so than the conduits. The use of the plural, 'conduits', also requires explanation.

It was not uncommon for the water requirements of a city to increase with rising population. Nowadays, such a need is often met by tapping a new source and directing the extra water into the mains supply, like a tributary, to supplement it. The normal Roman answer was to create a completely new, separate aqueduct, often running parallel to the existing

system but quite independent of it. Over the years a city thus often came to
be served by a number of different aqueducts. Lyon (Lugdunum) had four,
Pergamon ten (mostly Hellenistic), and Rome eleven. They may perhaps
best be summarised in a table, based on the work of G. Garbrecht (p. 142).[4]

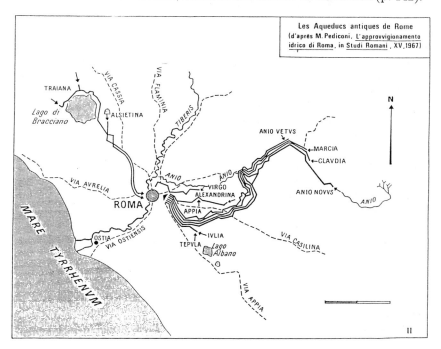

Fig. 48: Sketch map of the aqueducts of Rome.

As can be seen from the map (fig. 48), a number of these often followed
much the same course. In the case of Rome, most of them had their origins
in the Sabine hills, ran down the somewhat serpentine valley of the Anio
as far as Tivoli (Tibur), thence in a long loop southwards gradually losing
height to the level of the Campagna, across which they then ran straight in
to approach the city from the south-east, more or less along the line of the
Appian Way (from which, indeed, their arcades are prominently visible).
Potentially this could have been a very wasteful procedure architecturally,
necessitating a whole battery of similar arcades running alongside each
other. In fact this was avoided by a simple expedient: where a suitable
arcade already existed, the new conduit was built on top of it, and rode it

Table: The Aqueducts of Rome

	Year Built	Length of Conduit (in km)	Cross-section of Conduit (in m)	Height (m above sea-level) on Arrival in Rome	Volume of Discharge (m³ per 24 hrs)
Appia	312 BC	17.6	0.69 × 1.68	20	73,000
Anio Vetus	272	64	0.91 × 2.29	48	175,920
Marcia	144–40	91.2	1.52 × 2.59	59	187,600
Tepula	126	18.4	0.76 × 1.07	61	17,800
Julia	33	22.8	0.61 × 1.52	65	48,240
Virgo	21–19	20.8	0.61 × 1.75	20	100,160
Alsietina	10–2	32.8	1.75 × 2.59	17	15,680
Claudia	AD 38–52	68.8	0.91 × 1.98	67	184,280
Anio Novus		86.4	1.22 × 2.74	70	189,520
Traiana	109–117	59.2	1.30 × 2.29	73	113,920
Alexandriana	226	22.4	?	?	21,160
TOTAL* VOLUME FOR METROPOLITAN ROME					1,127,280

* individual and total discharge estimates, based on the figures of Frontinus, following P. Grimal.
Total as estimated by G. Garbrecht, 520,000–635,000.

piggy-back all the way to the city. The two building periods are often quite clearly distinct, construction methods having changed in the meantime. A good example is the long stretch of preserved arcade shown in pl. 36. This was built to carry the Aqua Claudia, the gaping rectangular mouth of which is prominently visible; the conduit and the arches supporting it are cut stone masonry. When, by A.D. 52, the Aqua Anio Novus was added on top, it was built of brick-faced concrete, and the addition stands out clearly as a separate layer. These superimposed conduits were built to a maximum of three, the Marcia (built 144 B.C.), Tepula (126 B.C.), and Julia (33 B.C.) being grouped together.

This solution did not come without its price. The original structure, not engineered to carry this extra load, sometimes could not cope with the strain. The cover slabs of the Marcia have often cracked under the weight of the Tepula and Julia built on top. Sometimes the arches themselves needed support, and one finds built inside the arch a second one of brick and concrete as a liner, to reinforce and support the original stone voussoirs (pl. 37). This did not always work, and occasionally one finds that the brick liner has settled more than the stone arch it is supposed to be supporting, leaving a clear gap between the two. Such strains normally manifested themselves outwardly in a series of leaks and spills, which must have been a standard feature of Roman aqueducts. Juvenal calls the Porta Capena 'dripping wet', *madida*, from leaks in the aqueduct passing above it; it was evidently notorious for it, since Martial says the same thing.[5] Used as we are to viewing the aqueducts as spectacular monuments, this practical aspect sometimes escapes us, and it took a modern hydraulic engineer, Clemens Herschel, to comment pointedly: 'The truth is, that these much vaunted works, whose *ruins* stand so long, were very poorly designed to *contain water*'.[6] Certainly, it is seldom pointed out that the endless series of inscriptions in which one emperor after another proudly announces how he has renovated and repaired such-and-such an aqueduct only emphasises how often and how readily they broke down.

The water was kept in separate channels because it came from different sources and was not all of the same quality. The Marcia was famous for its excellence—cool, clear and refreshing. The Tepula was tepid. The Julia was abundant, but sandy and impure. The Alsietina was muddy, unwholesome, fit only for watering gardens and supplying the *naumachia* (marine gladiatorial shows), and despised by everyone except the unfortunate residents of Trastevere, who, when the main supplies from the city were cut off for repairs to the Tiber bridges, had to drink it. In practice however this theoretical separation often broke down. Given the frequency (which seems to have been high) with which a part of the system would be shut down for repairs or maintenance, water often had to be diverted from its regular channel to serve an area that would otherwise go dry, and there must have been a whole series of crossover points, almost completely unknown to us, to facilitate re-routing and substitutions of this sort. The only limitations, since all the aqueducts did not arrive at Rome at the same level, was that, obviously, the water could only be diverted from a higher conduit into a lower one (see Table). Here the Tepula, with its supplies of poor-quality water, and built to run immediately on top of the Marcia, constituted a permanent temptation to the authorities: if the precious Marcia water was running short, what easier way than to help it out with an adulterating transfusion from the Tepula, and hope that nobody would notice? On the same principle, the Anio Novus, with its great volume of bad water, arriving in the city very high so that it could be fed into any of the others, was an even greater threat and invitation to abuse. Things could be made worse, and often were, by individual incompetence and corruption. When Frontinus took over he found that the theoretical separation of the aqueducts had largely broken down, leaving the distribution system a disorganised mess, where even the excellent Marcia water was sometimes being used, as he primly puts it, 'for purposes too foul to mention'.[7] It was largely by cleaning up such abuses that he made his name.

As one admires the endless march of the great arcades, one is yet sometimes assailed by a gnawing doubt: 'Why did they build them? Could this enormous expense not have been saved by something simpler, perhaps an earth embankment?'. One reasonable answer is that the arches did not impede the movement of surface water, so avoiding difficulties with drainage; another is that farmers across whose land the aqueduct ran thereby had easy access from one side to the other. No doubt they appreciated it, but one wonders whether just one or two crossing points would not suffice, rather than a non-stop continuum of arches. The same problem arose when railways were built across farms or estates, and there the occasional bridge or private crossing seems to have worked quite well. Probably the real reason is that we simply underestimate the labour involved in building a large embankment (which, to reach the 20m height of the Roman arches, would have needed a base of over 100m wide), forgetting that in the early days of railway construction, such as the London to Birmingham line, some of the great embankments were considered major engineering works in their own right. We also overestimate the difficulty to the Romans of building arcades. The form was repetitive, and concrete and brick construction was at the most a semi-skilled craft (under proper supervision). Moreover, the plan of an aqueduct, strung out in a long line, meant there was no limit to the number of work gangs that could get at it at once, unlike an amphitheatre or temple, which has to go up in stages as some parts have to be finished before others can be started. It will be remembered how in the mountain valleys siphons were where possible avoided, specifically because bridges were cheaper and easier to build.

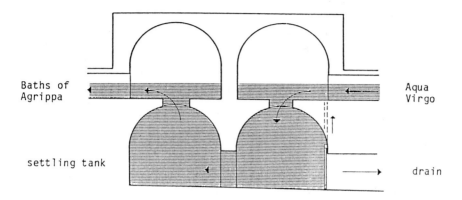

Fig. 49: Diagram of settling chamber on the Aqua Virgo, Rome.

On arrival at the city—at Rome all the eastern aqueducts arrived together at the Porta Maggiore (pl. 38); the channels of the Claudia and Anio Novus can be seen running above it—the aqueduct might be carried along the top of the city walls (as at Minturnae, Fréjus, and Orange) to a suitable distribution point. Filters, in our sense of the word, were extremely rare, but were often replaced by a series of settling chambers through which the water moved slowly, allowing sediment and detritus in suspension to settle to the bottom (fig. 49). In special cases the channel might then enter a large reception reservoir. Normally this was oblong and divided up by rows of piers, the aisles between them being roofed over by barrel vaults, so that in plan the whole structure looks rather like a basilica (fig. 50). The largest such classical cistern is the Bordj Djedid cistern at Carthage, with dimensions of 154.60m x 39 (the size of a city block) and a capacity of 30,000 cubic metres, and we may also note two in Campania, the 'Piscina Mirabilis' (66m x 25.45; 12,600 cubic metres) at Bacoli, possibly serving the needs of the fleet at Misenum, and the 'Cento Camerelle' serving a villa at Misenum and not yet fully excavated. Other examples of such reservoirs are to be noted at Lyon (15.75m x 14.05; 16,000 cubic metres) and a small one (2,000 cubic metres) at Chieti. The largest known, somewhat outside our period but still in use, is the enormous 'Cistern of the 1,001 Columns' in Istanbul, of early Byzantine date (140m x 70, 325,000 cubic metres), its vaulted roof sustained by Corinthian columns to the actual number of 336. Though impressive architecturally, these reservoirs could usually contain only about one day's output of the aqueduct they served (sometimes less), and were presumably intended to act as a buffer, taking up the quiet where either supply or demand were irregular; by filling up during the slack hours of the night they supplemented the aqueduct during day-time, enabling it to meet demands that would otherwise be too great for it. The Carthage cistern served the Antonine baths, where demand may have been greater by day. Such cisterns were therefore probably a first step toward regulating water use and away from the continuous offtake principle. Except in special cases or regions, they remained uncommon, and usually, on arrival, the water was fed directly into a *castellum divisorium*, or distribution tank.

Vitruvius describes one,[8] but his description is very confusingly expressed and it is in any case not clear whether he is even describing anything that actually existed or just giving his own personal advice and suggestions on what should be built. Various reconstructions of this device—its salient feature is that it is divided into three separate compartments, two of which overflow into the other—have been offered, but the reader must be warned that the question remains ambiguous and complicated. Of the actual *castella* found, the best-preserved are at Pompeii and Nîmes. Externally, the Pompeii one is unimpressive, being housed in a square brick building near the Porta Vesuvii, its walls bereft of any serious attempt at decoration. The hydraulic installation within is well-preserved, complex and peculiar, and may or may not reflect the specification of Vitruvius.

The Nîmes *castellum* (pl. 39) is simpler, but not innocent of architectural pretensions. Basically it is a shallow, open, round tank 6m across, built of masonry. At one side the aqueduct enters. At the other the water leaves through thirteen large (40cm diameter) lead pipes, ten in the side wall and three in the floor, on its way to various parts of the city. Today the site presents an aspect one can only call bleak, but the excavator's report makes it plain that in antiquity things were otherwise.[9] The tank, surrounded by a paved promenade with a bronze balustrade, was inside a small ceremonial building that must have looked like a shrine. Overhead was a tiled roof and on the lower parts of the walls were found traces of frescoes featuring dolphins and other appropriately aquatic themes. Plainly this was conceived as a place of public resort, where the citizens of Nîmes, out for an evening stroll, could lean over the balustrade and admire the waters swirling around below. The important thing here is not the preserved architecture, which is minimal, but the fact that part of a waterworks was

A

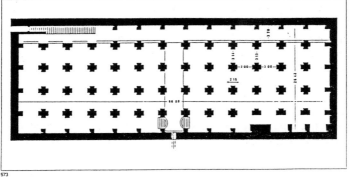

B

Fig. 50: Bacoli, near Naples: terminal storage reservoir known as the 'Piscina Mirabilis':
(a) drawing of remains by P. Gellier (late nineteenth century); (b) plan.

seen as a fit focus for civic pride, manifesting itself not only in architectural
embellishment but in public access. People were evidently expected to want
to go there and look at it. Other cities presumably may have felt the same
and celebrated their water supply in the same way, though no other similar
urban monument comes to mind. It is a feeling out of touch with modern
attitudes, where, except for large dams, which are inevitably and inherently
a public spectacle, the constituents of a water system are as a rule grimly
utilitarian. To catch the same feeling we have to go to something like the
eighteenth-century *château d'eau* du Peyrou at Montpellier, built by An-
toine Giral (pl. 40). The water approaches by crossing a valley on a long
and imposing Roman-type arcade, then, arriving on the plateau before the
city, enters the *château d'eau* (*castellum*), which takes the form of a small
but decorative hexagonal pavilion, in the Corinthian order, possibly based

on the Temple of Venus at Baalbek. An even more impressive example of the same attitude is to be seen in the great *Wasserturm* that forms the centrepiece of downtown Mannheim.

In its essence, this expresses much of what the citizens of Nîmes, and Romans in general, must have felt about water supply. For the same reason, the arcades and bridges were sometimes decorated. On the Gier aqueduct at Lyon, the arcades are faced with *opus reticulatum* in alternate black and white stones, giving a diagonal chessboard effect, with which the red brickwork of the arches combines to give a pleasingly polychrome appearance. It is perhaps ironic that the Romans, a people whom we complacently, even smugly, accuse of thinking meanly of technical matters, should in this vital field be more prompt than we are to a public recognition and celebration of monumental achievement.

For the reader wishing to pursue the matter further, we may close on a bibliographical note. Study of aqueducts, as in most fields of ancient technology, is a classic example of falling between two stools. Classicists are understandably reluctant to embark upon the technical aspects, unqualified to do so, and often unreliable when they try to. Engineers are only rarely interested in history, lacking in ancient historical background, and unable to read the Latin of the relevant texts such as Frontinus. The definitive account of Roman aqueducts thus remains yet to be written. Perhaps, given the present organisation of our scholarship, it cannot be. Because of this, aqueduct study has up to the present been strongly slanted in two ways. First, it has concentrated on the aqueducts of Rome itself, and although these did constitute the most splendid example of Roman aqueduct building, they were not always typical of practice elsewhere; in particular, it has led to the underestimation of two features rarely found at Rome, siphons and dams. Second, there has been a strong archaeological bias, with a great deal of attention placed on dating and brick stamps and relatively little on how the aqueducts worked. However, it is precisely this feature that many students find most interesting, with the result that in Thomas Ashby's monumental work *The Aqueducts of Rome* the most frequently consulted chapter is the very short one entitled 'The Engineering of the Aqueducts', not because it is particularly good—it is not—but because it is all there is on that topic that is easily found and accessible. This situation is changing, as the increasing stress on social history also leads to an increasing interest in the technological aspects of antiquity. In aqueduct studies, at least, this new and potentially fruitful approach to these structures seems to be centred mainly in Germany, where two learned associations, the Frontinus Gesellschaft and the Leichtweiss Institut für Wasserbau, Brunswick, have done much to forward our understanding of them.

NOTES

1. Frontinus, *Aqueducts* 16. The most convenient text and translation of Frontinus is by C.E. Bennett in the Loeb Classical Library (London 1925). For a fuller commentary, in French, see the excellent edition by P. Grimal, *Frontin* (Budé ed., Paris 1961).

2. Wheeler, *Roman Art and Architecture* (1964), 16.

3. E.g. Ward-Perkins, *Roman Imperial Architecture* (1981), 303.

4. Garbrecht, *Wasserversorgung im antiken Rom* (1986), 33.

5. Juvenal 3.11; Martial 3.47.1.

6. Herschel, *The Two Books ... of Sextus Julius Frontinus* (1913), 231.

7. Frontinus, *Aqueducts* 91.

8. 8.6.1f.

9. *Les Archives de la Commission des Monuments Historiques* (Paris 1855–72), vol.I, p.1; André Nadal, *Le Castellum* (Nîmes 1974), 55, confirms that during the nineteenth century outlines of fishes and dolphins, now disappeared, were still discernible.

Afterword: the Theatre of Civic Life

T.P. Wiseman

At the end of its circuitous fourteen-mile course, the Aqua Virgo emerged from beneath the Collis Hortulorum (the modern Pincio) and was carried across the Tiber flood-plain to feed Agrippa's Baths and the fountains of the Augustan Campus Martius. It crossed the Via Flaminia at right-angles, marking off, like a city wall, the grassy meadows of the Campus proper from the splendid townscape created by Pompey, Augustus and Agrippa himself. The arch over the road, like a city gate, was decorated by Claudius as the triumphal monument of his British victory.

What the aqueduct looked like was revealed in the early seventeenth century, when the foundations were being dug for the church of S. Ignazio. A contemporary report described the remains:[1]

> The piers were faced with marble slabs on the outside, with *antae* of Corinthian columns at the side: while the pilasters were a little drawn back (recessed), and were also faced with marble. The epistyles, friezes, and cornices were of marble, while statues stood, I think, on the fluted marble columns. In the interior the piers were strengthened with travertine, with Doric pilasters supporting the epistyle and the cornice. Above these was brickwork, in which the *specus* was carried: it was about 6 palms high, and 3 wide (1.33 x 0.67m). The arches between the piers were faced with marble.

That elaborate architectural ornament resembles nothing so much as the *scaenae frons* of a Roman theatre—and I think that is not just a coincidence.

We must not draw too schematic a distinction between the various categories of Roman public buildings and the purposes for which they were designed. In this very area of the southern Campus Martius (fig. 51), we have the Circus Flaminius, by name a 'place of entertainment', but in fact a piazza for markets and public meetings (though shows could be staged there, and sometimes were); we have the great theatre of Pompey, with its temple of Venus Victrix and its portico that incorporated a Senate-house (the one where Caesar was murdered, cf. p. 79); we have the Saepta, voting enclosures for the Roman citizens' assembly, superbly adorned with a huge colonnade and used, among other things, for exhibitions, gladiatorial combats and mock sea battles. A contemporary description of the Augustan complex tells us that the marvellous buildings and their Campus setting 'present to the eye the appearance of a stage-painting, offering a spectacle one can hardly draw away from'.[2] Where, one might ask, does theatre end and real life—public life—begin?

From the very beginnings of the classical world, spectacle and public life were inseparable—the dancing place and the judgement place were both in the *agora*. And when the Greeks began to build theatres, they used them for discussing politics as well as for watching performances. The theatre, like the *agora* (and often they were the same thing), was the meeting-place of the community for whatever concerned it as a community, whether political, judicial or religious (for dance and drama were of course in honour of the gods). In fact, the categories are anachronistic: *everything* that happened there was 'political', in the sense that it was of the *polis*.[3]

Within limits, the same applied to Rome. The Forum saw not only citizens' assemblies, and magistrates haranguing public meetings, but also, on festival days, gladiators, boxers, tightrope-walkers, and plays like the *Hecyra* of Terence, vainly trying to compete. There is a passage in Plautus, analysing the various specialities of the Forum crowd, which was surely written for a performance in the Forum itself.[4] The architectural development of the Forum confirms the literary evidence. As early as the fourth century B.C., balconies were constructed above the shops to provide a better view for spectators;[5] the later basilicas, to judge by the famous coin representation of the Basilica Aemilia, were built two storeys high for the same reason; and Caesar even planned to construct a huge theatre-auditorium up against the Tarpeian Rock, overlooking the Forum from the Capitol end.[6]

It is true that the Romans strongly resisted using purpose-built theatres for political meetings in the Greek style,[7] but much of what went

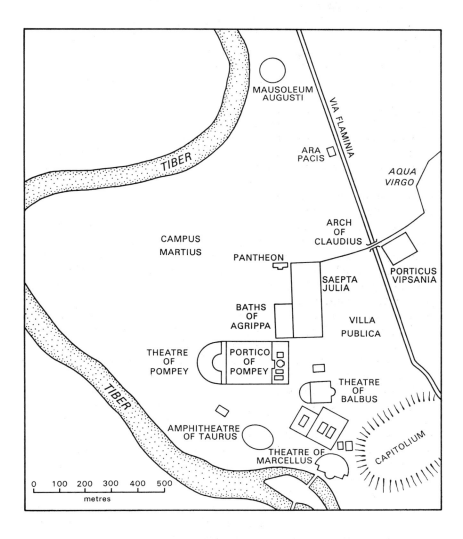

Fig. 51: Plan of the Campus Martius, showing Agrippa's developments.

on in the theatres during the *ludi scaenici* was very political in the more general sense. Popular politicians were applauded, unpopular ones were hissed; the actors deliberately played up lines that could be given a topical reference; indeed, Cicero tells us that demonstrations in the theatre were an important index of popular feeling.[8] No doubt the same applied at the Circus Maximus during the *ludi circenses*, though for that our best evidence comes from the principate, when it is quite clear that the games provided an occasion for the emperor to show himself to the people, and for the people to express their loyalty or voice their complaints.[9]

Public life, or spectacle? The two categories cannot be separated. According to Seneca, the Saepta, the Forum and the Circus were where you would see the greatest crowds in Rome, 'and as many vices as there are men'.[10] It would clearly be unreal to classify them too rigidly as different types of place, designed for different types of activity. Life in the Roman world was not so compartmentalised.

Imagine the scene when the great man's doors are opened for the morning *salutatio*. The clients flood into the *atrium*, gaping at the tortoiseshell inlay and the Corinthian bronzes.[11] It is a spectacle; and so is the procession down to the Forum, and the parade up and down the length of the basilica.[12] As for the issues of high politics, they are a play, a performance, as Cicero, for instance, described the trial of Clodius, or Cluvius Rufus the death of Caligula.[13] The letters of Marcus Caelius to Cicero are particularly revealing, for their consistent view of politics as *spectaculum* and *scaena*.[14]

According to Cicero, you could always tell when a real orator was in action in the Forum, even if you were too far away to know what the case was about: the big crowd round the tribunal, hushed and spellbound, told you that 'Roscius was on the stage'.[15] Even when politics collapsed into civil war, with legionary battles in the streets of Rome, the citizens were still an applauding audience—as if, says Tacitus, they were watching gladiators at the games.[16] And the 'theatre' of this continuous spectacle was the city and its public buildings, a backdrop worthy of the drama that was played before it.

Augustus, on his deathbed, asked his friends 'Have I played my part properly?'[17] That may serve as the last word of a book in which Augustus, for good reason, has loomed large. For he not only played his part; he rebuilt the theatre as well.

NOTES

1. T. Ashby, *The Aqueducts of Ancient Rome* (Oxford 1935), 181, translating Donati, *Roma vetus ac recens* (1638), 292.

2. Strabo 5.236.

3. See F. Kolb, *Agora und Theater, Volks- und Festversammlung* (Berlin 1981), esp. ch. 6, 'Theater und Volksversammlung'. In Apuleius' *Golden Ass* (3.2-10), Lucius at Larisa finds himself put on trial in the theatre.

4. See E.J. Jory, CQ 36 (1986), 537–9, and M. Gaggiotti, *Analecta Romana* 14 (1985), 60, on Plautus, *Curculio* 470-82. On a 'conducted tour' of the Forum, the audience is told where to find 'people of every kind ... vicious or virtuous, worthy or worthless': perjurers, boastful liars, spendthrifts, prostitutes and their clients, members of dining clubs, respectable wealthy citizens, show-offs, malicious gossipers, moneylenders and 'behind the Temple of Castor, people that you'd better not trust in a hurry'. The 'virtuous and worthy' are clearly in a minority.

5. Festus 120L.

6. Suetonius, *Divus Julius* 44.1.

7. Cicero, *pro Flacco* 15f.

8. *pro Sestio* 115–26. Examples from the late Republic: Plutarch, *Cicero* 13 (63 B.C.); Cicero, *ad Atticum* 1.16.11 (61 B.C.); 2.19.3 (59 B.C.); *in Pisonem* 65 (55 B.C.); *ad Atticum* 4.15.6 (54 B.C.); *ad familiares* 8.2.1 (51 B.C.); *ad Atticum* 14.3.2 and *Philippic* 1.37 (44 B.C.). For the Augustan age, cf. Propertius 3.18.17–20; Horace, *Odes* 1.20.2-8; 2.17.25f.

9. See A. Cameron, *Circus Factions* (Oxford 1976), esp. ch. 7, 'The Emperor and his People at the Games'.

10. *de ira* 2.8.1.

11. Virgil, *Georgics* 2.461-4.

12. Cicero, *pro Murena* 70.

13. Cicero, *ad Atticum* 1.18.2, 'introitus fuit fabulae Clodianae' ('the Clodian drama came on the stage'); Josephus, *Jewish Antiquities* 19.92, cf. 199, 'teleiosis tou dramatos' ('final act of the drama'). Cf. Cicero, *de amicitia* 97 for the public meeting as a stage performance ('in scaena, id est in contione'); also *in Verrem* 5.35; *ad Quintum fratrem* 1.1.42; *pro Rabirio Postumo* 42 for service in the provinces as performance in the theatre.

14. Cicero, *ad familiares* 8.4.1; 11.1; 14.1, 4.

15. *Brutus* 290.

16. *Histories* 3.83.1.

17. Suetonius, *Divus Augustus* 99.1.

Glossary

aedes: a temple building

aedicula (lit. 'small shrine'): a recess or niche in a wall, usually framed with columns and a pediment

agora: (Gr.) a market-place; the centre of civic life in a Greek *polis*

amphitheatre: a building for shows with seating all round

antae: pilasters terminating the side walls of a temple building

apodyterium: the changing-room of a bath building

apse: a semicircular recess in a wall (usually the end wall) of a building, often roofed with a half-dome

arcade: a continuous series of arches

arch: a structural device in which the downward thrust is distributed to solid supports at either side; in Roman architecture usually semicircular in form, but flat arches are occasionally found

architrave: the cross-beam above a row of columns

arena (Lat. *harena* 'sand'): the area in which the shows of the amphitheatre took place

arx: a citadel; the highest point of a town, corresponding to Gr. *acropolis*

atrium: the main central room of a Roman house; also applied to similar rooms in public buildings

augur: a priest whose function was to observe and interpret the flight of birds for purposes of divination

balneum: a simple suite of baths, public or private (cf. *thermae*)

basilica: a rectangular hall used for law-courts and other public business

caldarium: the hot room of a bath building

carceres (lit. 'prisons'): the starting gates for chariot races in a circus

cardo (lit. 'hinge'): the north-south line of a surveyor's grid; in modern usage, applied to the north-south streets of a town, the main one being the *cardo maximus*. The corresponding term for east-west streets is *decumanus*

castellum: a water-tank into which an aqueduct discharged, and from which water was distributed to various parts of a town

cavea: the auditorium of a theatre or amphitheatre

cella: the main chamber of a temple, containing the cult statue; some temples have more than one

circus: a place for chariot races, but also used for other spectacles

colonia: originally a military settlement of Roman citizens, usually in conquered territory; later, the highest grade of municipal status, in which all the burgesses obtained Roman citizenship

colonnade: a row of columns, usually fronting a covered walk

column: a post, normally circular in section, supporting an entablature (q.v.). A rectangular support is normally referred to as a pillar

comitium: the place of assembly for the citizen body, at Rome or elsewhere

cornice: the highest member of the entablature, immediately below the roof

cunei (lit. 'wedges'): the blocks of seats in a theatre or amphitheatre

curia: the place of meeting of the Senate at Rome and of town councils elsewhere

decumanus: see *cardo*

dome: the hemispherical roof of a circular or polygonal building

engaged: term applied to columns which partially project from a wall

entablature: all that part of an Order (q.v.) which comes above the columns; it regularly consists of three parts: architrave, frieze and cornice

exedra: a recess, often with seats, either semicircular or rectangular in plan

forum: an open space in a town, used as a market place or civic centre, like the Greek *agora*

frieze: a continuous horizontal band resting on the architrave, either left plain or decorated with relief carving

frigidarium: the cold room of a bath building

hexastyle: having six columns on the façade

insula (lit. 'island'): a block of flats or apartment house; in modern usage, applied to any city block surrounded by streets

intercolumniation: the space between two adjacent columns

laconicum: a dry hot room in a bath building, like a modern sauna

macellum: a market, strictly for meat, but extended to other foodstuffs

maenianum: a tier of seats in an amphitheatre

meta: a turning-post at either end of the *spina* (q.v.) in a circus

modillions: horizontal brackets supporting the projecting cornice in the Corinthian Order

municipium: originally an Italian town which had received Roman citizenship; later, the second grade of municipal status, in which only magistrates (or sometimes all councillors) obtained Roman citizenship

natatio: a swimming pool

nymphaeum: an ornamental fountain

octastyle: having eight columns on the façade

oculus (lit. 'eye'): a circular opening at the top of a dome

odeum (Gr. *odeion*): a small roofed theatre for musical and other recitals

opus: a style of construction, particularly applied to the facing of walls: *opus quadratum*, large stone slabs cut square and laid horizontally; *opus incertum*, irregular small pieces of stone; *opus reticulatum*, small squared blocks of regular size laid diagonally in a network pattern

orchestra (Gr. 'dancing place'): the part of a theatre at the bottom of the cavea, in front of the stage

order: a system of parts, including its proportions and the style of its decoration, originally developed in building the columns and entablatures of Greek temples. The three classical Orders are Doric, Ionic and Corinthian

palaestra: an exercise ground

parodoi: the entrance passage to the orchestra (q.v.) of the Greek theatre

pediment: the triangular space on the façade of a building formed by the gable end of a pitched roof above the horizontal entablature

peripteral: having columns all round

peristyle: an open courtyard or garden surrounded by colonnades

pilaster: an engaged (q.v.) pillar

pillar: see *column*

podium: the raised platform on which a Roman temple stands

pomerial: term applied to a road running round inside the defences of a fort or town (from *pomerium*, the formal boundary of Rome and of other Latin cities)

porticus: a covered walk or colonnade; also applied to a set of colonnades surrounding the area in which a building (or buildings) stands

praecinctio: a horizontal gangway in a theatre or amphitheatre

pronaos (Gr.): the entrance porch of a temple

propylon (Gr.): a monumental gateway; also in the plural form *propylaea*

prostyle: having a row of columns in front

pseudodipteral: peripteral (q.v.), but with the columns positioned so far out from the walls of the cella that there would have been room for an additional row of columns

pseudoperipteral: having columns engaged in the side and rear walls

pulpitum: the stage of a theatre; its front wall, above the orchestra

rotunda: a building of circular plan

scaena: the building (sometimes only a wall) at the back of the stage in a theatre; its wall facing the audience is called the *scaenae frons*

sine postico (lit. 'without a back part'): Vitruvius' term for a temple which is peripteral on three sides only

siphon (inverted): a device for bringing water in pipes downhill and returning it to near its original level

soffit: the exposed underside of an architectural member (architrave, cornice etc.)

specus: the conduit of an aqueduct

spina: a term used by many modern authorities to denote the longitudinal wall separating the two sides of the race-track in a circus *stoa* (Gr.): a colonnade (= Lat. *porticus*)

stylobate: the level platform on which columns stand; in Roman temples, the top of the podium (q.v.)

tabernae: shops

temenos (Gr.): a sacred enclosure (= Lat. *templum*)

tepidarium: the warm room of a bath building

tetrastyle: having four columns on the façade

theatre: a place for dramatic performances, usually semicircular in plan

thermae: a large public bath building

tholos (Gr.): a temple-like round building

travertine: a kind of limestone quarried near Tivoli, much used (in ancient and modern times) for building in Rome

triglyph: a plaque decorated with vertical grooves, characteristic of the Doric frieze

vault: an arched roof covering a passage or room. The main types employed in Roman architecture are the barrel-vault, which is in effect an arch moved along a straight line; the cross-vault, formed by the intersection of two barrel-vaults; and the dome (q.v.)

venter: the horizontal run of an aqueduct at the bottom of a siphon (q.v.)

versurae: walls projecting from the end of the *scaena* (q.v.) to connect it with the *cavea* (q.v.)

vomitorium: a passage giving access to and from the seats in the *cavea* (q.v.) of a theatre or amphitheatre

Guide to Further Reading

There are several general books on Roman architecture which give good accounts of the subject. Still useful, although it first appeared nearly sixty years ago, is D.S. Robertson, *Greek and Roman Architecture* (2nd edition, Cambridge 1943—often reprinted); it is of particular value to anyone who wishes to compare Roman buildings with their Greek antecedents. So, in its own idiosyncratic way, is H. Plommer, *Ancient and Classical Architecture* (London 1956). For Roman architecture itself, the best general handbook in English is that published in 1970 in the Pelican History of Art series under the title *Etruscan and Roman Architecture*, consisting of two parts which have since been republished separately: A. Boëthius, *Etruscan and Early Roman Architecture* (Harmondsworth 1978), and J.B. Ward-Perkins, *Roman Imperial Architecture* (Harmondsworth 1981). A shorter book, with fewer detailed discussions of individual buildings, but with some good descriptions of design and construction, is F. Sear, *Roman Architecture* (London 1982). There are useful photographs, plans and reconstructions in F.E. Brown, *Roman Architecture* (London/New York 1961) and in G.C. Picard, *Living Architecture: Roman* (London 1965). A comprehensive treatment, with many useful photographs and plans, is a volume of the Italian Enciclopedia classica: L. Crema, *L'architettura romana* (Torino 1959). Two important American publications should also be mentioned: the three volumes by M.E. Blake, *Roman Construction in Italy* (Washington 1947, 1959, 1973), which deal fully with the technical aspects of building from the prehistoric period to the Antonine Empire, and W.L. MacDonald, *The Architecture of the Roman Empire* (New Haven 1965, 1986), whose second volume 'An Urban Appraisal' gives generous treatment to the public urban architecture of the Empire. Finally, there is a descriptive catalogue of Roman sites by G.M. Woloch in the English translation of P. Grimal, *Roman Cities* (Madison, Wisconsin 1983).

T.W. Potter, *Roman Italy* (London 1987)—the first of a new series by British Museum Publications under the general title 'Exploring the Roman World'—is an accessible and up-to-date study, of which Chapter 4 'Cities and urbanisation' deals with some of the major themes of this book. The fundamental study of ancient town-planning is F. Castagnoli, *Orthogonal Town Planning in Antiquity* (Cambridge, Mass./London 1971), on which is based the admirable concise treatment by J.B. Ward-Perkins, *Cities of Ancient Greece and Italy* (London 1974). Important aspects of urban development under the Republic and early Empire are treated in F.E. Brown, *Cosa: the making of a Roman town* (Ann Arbor 1980); R. Meiggs, *Roman Ostia* (2nd edition, Oxford 1973); F. Coarelli, 'Public buildings in Rome between the Second Punic War and Sulla', PBSR 45 (1977), 1-23; J.B. Ward-Perkins, 'From Republic to Empire: reflections on the early provincial architecture of the Roman West', JRS 60 (1970), 1-19. Two foreign-language studies centre on the theme of the impact of Greek culture on central Italy in the last two centuries of the Republic: P. Gros, *Architecture et société à Rome et en Italie centre-meridionale* (Bruxelles 1978), and P. Zanker (ed.), *Hellenismus in Mittelitalien* (Groningen 1976).

For discussion of civic and other buildings it is usually necessary to go to reports on individual sites (see below), but there are special studies of baths and markets: E. Brodner, *Die römischen Thermen und das antike Badewesen* (Darmstadt 1983), and C. de Ruyt, *Macellum: marché alimentaire des romains* (Louvain 1983).

There is no full treatment of religious buildings in English. The standard work is H. Kähler, *Der römischer Tempel* (Berlin 1970), and two particular groups are examined by J.A. Hanson, *Roman Theater-Temples* (Princeton 1959), and by I.M. Barton, 'Capitoline Temples in Italy and the provinces (especially Africa)', ANRW 2.12.1 (1981), 259-342. J.E. Stambaugh, 'The functions of Roman temples', ANRW 2.16.1 (1978), 554-608, is a useful survey, and Chapter 8 'Gods and their temples' of T.W. Potter's book (above) is excellent on the cults of Italy.

The most comprehensive treatment of theatres is M. Bieber, *The History of the Greek and Roman Theater* (2nd edition, Princeton 1961). See also E. Frézouls, 'Aspects de l'histoire architecturale du théâtre romain', ANRW 2.12.1 (1981), 343-441. The spectacles that took place in amphitheatres are described in J. Pearson, *Arena: the story of the Colosseum* (London 1973). There is a detailed study of circuses by J.H. Humphrey, *Roman Circuses: arenas for chariot racing* (London 1986). The mechanics, organisation and social significance of chariot-racing are succinctly discussed in the third part of H.A. Harris, *Sport in Greece and Rome* (London 1972).

The topic of water supply has an important bibliography of its own, but much earlier discussion is now out of date. The author of our Chapter Five has written a book on the subject: A.T. Hodge, *Roman Aqueducts and Water Supply* (London 1989). Easily the best illustrations are to be found in G. Garbrecht (ed.), *Wasserversorgung im antiken Rom* (München/Wien 1986). R.J. Forbes, *Studies in Ancient Technology*, vol. 1 (Leiden 1964), Chapter 3 (pp. 149-194), is comprehensive but of varying reliability. Two older, but still important, books are E. Van Deman, *The Building of the Roman Aqueducts* (Washington 1934)—highly technical, concentrating on building materials, dating and construction methods—and T. Ashby, *The Aqueducts of Ancient Rome* (Oxford 1935)—a meticulous and comprehensive record of the remains of the aqueducts of metropolitan Rome, but the exposition is often confusing to the beginner.

Most of the works cited in the foregoing paragraphs include bibliographies, more or less detailed, which should be consulted for further information, especially on the site reports which underlie the advances in knowledge of recent years, many of which are by European scholars writing in their own languages. There are also some important monographs on individual buildings or groups of buildings; and—if written by scholars from first-hand knowledge—site guides, especially some of the Italian ones, can be very valuable. The following is only a brief, and arbitrary, selection:

ROME

F. Coarelli, *Roma* (Milano 1980): well illustrated guide

P. Zanker, *Forum Augustum: das Bildprogramm* (Tübingen 1968)

K. de F. Licht, *The Rotunda in Rome: a study of Hadrian's Pantheon* (Copenhagen 1966): a very detailed survey, covering all aspects

W.L. MacDonald, *The Pantheon: design, meaning, and progeny* (London 1976): a more general account, in the series 'The Architect and Society'

MacDonald also has detailed treatments of Trajan's Market and the Pantheon in the first volume of his work cited in the first paragraph above.

For any extant building in Rome, excellent photographs and full bibliographies will be found in E. Nash, *Pictorial Dictionary of Ancient Rome*, two volumes (2nd edition, London 1968).

ITALY

For Cosa and Ostia, see the works cited in the second paragraph above.

J. Mertens, *Alba Fucens* (Bruxelles 1981): excavation report in French

G.A. Mansuelli, 'Marzabotto, dix années de fouilles et de recherches', MEFR 84 (1972), 111-144

F. Fasolo and G. Gullini, *Il santuario di Fortuna Primigenia a Palestrina* (Roma 1953)

A. and M. De Vos, *Pompei, Ercolano, Stabia* (Roma/Bari 1982): guide, copiously illustrated, in the Italian Laterza series

PROVINCES

S.J. Keay, *Roman Spain* (London 1988): the second volume in the British Museum series mentioned above (p. 164). Further volumes are announced on Gaul and Germany, Britain, Turkey and North Africa.

B. Cunliffe, *Roman Bath discovered* (London 1971)

E.M. Wightman, *Roman Trier and the Treveri* (London 1970)

R. Amy and P. Gros, *La Maison Carrée de Nîmes* (Paris 1979)

M.F. Squarciapino, *Lepcis Magna* (Basel 1966): in German

F. Ragette, *Baalbek* (London 1980)

I. Browning, *Jerash and the Decapolis* (London 1982)

For brief descriptions and bibliographies of individual sites, consult *The Princeton Encyclopaedia of Classical Sites* (Princeton 1976) or articles in *Enciclopedia dell'arte antica, classica e orientale* (Roma 1958–66).

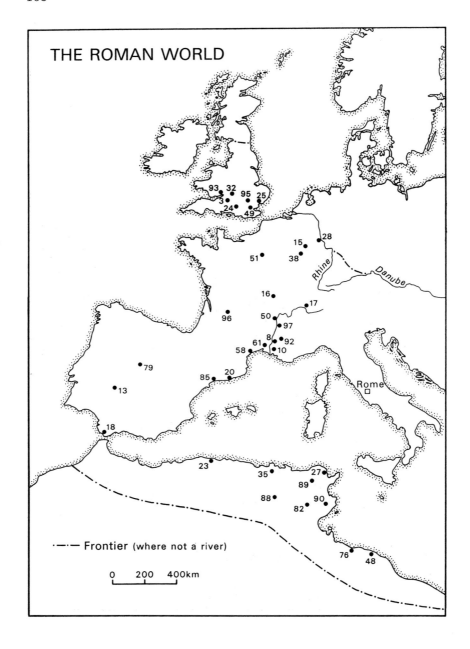

THE ROMAN WORLD

—·— Frontier (where not a river)

0   200   400km

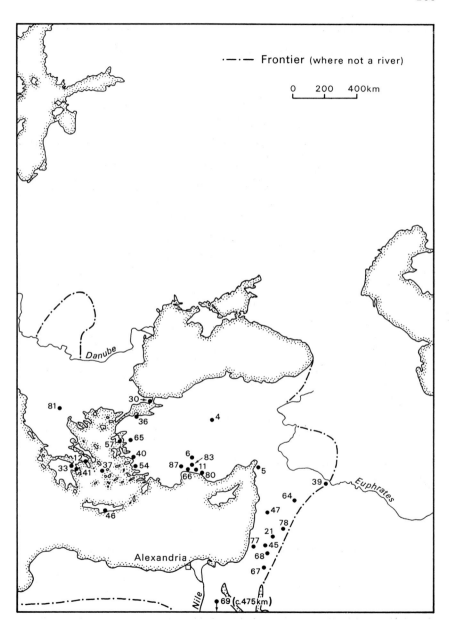

Frontier (where not a river)

0   200   400km

Danube

81•

30•

36•

4•

57•   •65

•12   •40   54•

33•   •41   37•   •54

87•   6•   •83

66•   11•   •80

5•

39•   Euphrates

64•

•47

78•

21•

77•   •45

•68

67•

Alexandria

Nile

•69 (c.475km)

46•

Index of Sites and Buildings

(NOTE — All sites are listed under their ancient name where this is known, with cross-reference from the modern name if this differs significantly. The numbers against the names of sites provide a key to the maps.)

Notes on Contributors

Ian M. Barton read Classics at Corpus Christi College, Cambridge, and after lecturing at Keele and in Ghana went to Saint David's University College, Lampeter, where he was until recently Head of the Department of Classics. His special interests include classical art and architecture and Roman imperial history, especially that of North Africa. He is the author of *Africa in the Roman Empire.*

A.J. Brothers, a graduate of The Queen's College, Oxford, is Senior Lecturer in Classics at Saint David's University College, Lampeter, where his lecturing commitments include Roman architecture. His chief research interest is Roman comedy (particularly Terence), but he has also published articles on Roman architecture and religion. He frequently acts as lecturer and guide at classical sites around the Mediterranean.

John Carter read Classics at Corpus Christi College, Cambridge, and went on to lecture on classical art and architecture at Melbourne University before taking up his present post at Royal Holloway and Bedford New College, London, where he specialises in the history of the late Republican and Augustan periods.

A. Trevor Hodge was born in Belfast and read Classics at Gonville and Caius College, Cambridge, where he obtained a Ph.D. for his study of the woodwork of Greek roofs. Since 1960 he has taught at Carleton University, Ottawa, where he is a full Professor. His principal current research interests are Roman water supply (on which a book is forthcoming) and the Greek colonisation of the South of France.

E.J. Owens was educated at Liverpool Collegiate School and Sheffield University, where he undertook research for M.A. and Ph.D. He was a Junior Research Fellow at Sheffield before taking up his present appointment at University College, Swansea, in 1978. His main interests lie in Roman Republican history and Graeco-Roman archaeology, and he is preparing a book on Roman town planning.

T.P. Wiseman is Professor of Classics at the University of Exeter. His books include *New Men in the Roman Senate* (1971), *Clio's Cosmetics* (1979), *Catullus and his World* (1985) and *Roman Studies* (1987).